JOURNAL FOR THE STUDY OF THE OLD TESTAMENT
SUPPLEMENT SERIES
203

Sheffield Academic Press

Spikenard and Saffron

The Imagery of the Song of Songs

Jill M. Munro

Journal for the Study of the Old Testament
Supplement Series 203

For Mary

Published by Sheffield Academic Press Ltd
Mansion House
19 Kingfield Road
Sheffield, S11 9AS
England

Printed on acid-free paper in Great Britain
by Bookcraft Ltd
Midsomer Norton, Bath

British Library Cataloguing in Publication Data

A catalogue record for this book is available
from the British Library

ISBN 1-85075-562-0

CONTENTS

ACKNOWLEDGMENTS

This study was first presented as a doctoral dissertation at the University of Edinburgh in 1991. It was written under the supervision of Professor J.C.L. Gibson, whose encouragement sustained me in my work at every stage along the way. To him I owe the deepest debt of gratitude.

For his incisive remarks and careful reading of the text, I also thank Dr N. Wyatt, who gave most generously of his time on my behalf.

Finally, to my family and friends who encouraged and cajoled, and without whom neither thesis nor book would have reached completion, my sincere appreciation.

ABBREVIATIONS

AASOR	Annual of American Schools of Oriental Research
AB	Anchor Bible
AJSL	*American Journal of Semitic Languages and Literatures*
AnBib	Analecta biblica
ANEP	J.B. Pritchard (ed.), *Ancient Near East in Pictures*
ANET	J.B. Pritchard (ed.), *Ancient Near Eastern Texts*
AOAT	Alter Orient und Altes Testament
AOS	American Oriental Series
ASTI	*Annual of the Swedish Theological Institute*
Bib	*Biblica*
BibOr	Biblica et orientalia
BKAT	Biblischer Kommentar: Altes Testament
BZ	*Biblische Zeitschrift*
BZAW	Beihefte zur *ZAW*
CBQ	*Catholic Biblical Quarterly*
CT	W.G. Lambert (ed.), Cuneiform Texts from Babylonian Tablets in the British Museum.
ETL	*Ephemerides theologicae lovanienses*
FOTL	The Forms of the Old Testament Literature
GKC	*Gesenius' Hebrew Grammar*, ed. E. Kautzsch, trans. A.E. Cowley
IB	*Interpreter's Bible*
Int	Interpretation
JBL	*Journal of Biblical Literature*
JCS	*Journal of Cuneiform Studies*
JQR	*Jewish Quarterly Review*
JSOT	*Journal for the Study of the Old Testament*
JSOTSup	*Journal for the Study of the Old Testament*, Supplement Series
JSS	*Journal of Semitic Studies*
JTS	*Journal of Theological Studies*
KAT	Kommentar zum Alten Testament
KTU	M. Dietrich, O. Loretz and J. Sammartín (eds.), *Keilalphabetischen Texte aus Ugarit*
LD	Lectio divina
OBO	Orbis biblicus et orientalis
Or	*Orientalia*
OTG	Old Testament Guides
PEQ	*Palestine Exploration Quarterly*
RA	*Revue d'assyriologie et d'archéologie orientale*

RB	*Revue biblique*
RSR	*Recherches de science religieuse*
SJT	*Scottish Journal of Theology*
SR	*Studies in Religion/Sciences religieuses*
UF	*Ugarit-Forschungen*
VT	*Vetus Testamentum*
ZAW	*Zeitschrift für die alttestamentliche Wissenschaft*
ZDMG	*Zeitschrift der deutschen morgenländischen Gesellschaft*

INTRODUCTION

The Song of Songs has in every age moved its readers by its imaginative power. Although, in the history of its exegesis, there are few studies of the imagery of the Song for its own sake, images are an essential element in the constitution of the Song and every exegesis must take account of them. Leaving aside, therefore, questions of authorship, date, provenance and literary history, questions which are still much debated by scholars, it is to the imagery that I directly turn, and in particular to a discussion of the way in which the various interpretations of the Song deal with this important aspect of the poem.

The allegorical reading is undoubtedly the most exploited in the history of the Song's exegesis and the approach which has beyond all others reflected upon the theological or spiritual import of individual metaphors. In the course of the early centuries of our era, under the influence of Hellenistic philosophy, this approach became predominant, as verses and sometimes individual words of the Song were used to formulate a variety of traditional teaching. By the early Middle Ages, not only were there three midrashim devoted to the Song (*Canticles Rabbah*, *Aggadat Shir Hashirim* and *Midrash Shir Hashirim*), but the Targum too provided a commentary on the Song, reading it as a sequence depicting the history of Israel from the exodus to the coming of the messiah.

Conceived in Jewish circles in the early centuries of our era, the allegorical interpretation profoundly influenced Christian writers, who at that time were beginning to elaborate an ecclesiology. Origen, in particular, saw the relationship between the imagery of the Song and the nuptial imagery of the New Testament (Mt. 9.15; 25.1-3; Jn 3.29; 2 Cor. 11.2; Eph. 5.22-23; Rev. 19.6-8; 21.9-11; 22.17) and in his commentary on the Song, written between 240 and 245 CE, he consistently identifies the woman with the church, and her lover with Christ. Like Hippolytus (d. 235) before him, he was not unaware of the plain sense of the Song which he considered to be a marriage epithalamium in dramatic form. Its

importance however lay in the theological truths to which it gave access
by means of symbols and figures.

The interpretations proffered by Origen were developed in a variety
of ways in patristic and medieval periods. Throughout that time, words
from the Song are mentioned whenever they are suitable for evoking
the central experiences of the spiritual life, for elucidating something of
the mystery of faith. They are to be found in hymns, letters, homilies
and commentaries and, with particular density, in the baptismal
catechisms of Ambrose and Cyril.[1] In these fourth-century liturgies, it is
the mystical dimension which predominates. In the spiritual writings of
Gregory of Nyssa and Bernard of Clairvaux, it is instead the moral or
spiritual interpretation which comes to the fore.

The allegorical interpretation has survived, though with fewer
adherents, in the twentieth century. Among those who do favour this
reading are Joüon (1909) and Robert, Tournay and Feuillet (1963), who
follow the targumic interpretation which sees Yahweh and Israel as the
chief protagonists. A particularly interesting development of this interpretation is proposed by Tournay (1988) who suggests that the protagonists are Israel and the hoped-for messiah. He relates the themes of
seeking and finding, of absence and presence, to the experience of the
exile.

The allegorical interpretation in its various forms is a venerable
tradition which, so far from being cold and mechanistic, is extremely
supple. Its strength lies in its capacity to stimulate the imagination to
explore the very parameters of faith. In so doing it discloses the spiritual
and theological depths of a particular worldview, Jewish or Christian.
The disadvantage however is that the Song is in danger of becoming a
code to be cracked, a means to an end, for the vivid imagery of the
Song tends to be subordinated to a general interpretation in the light of
which the Song as an imaginative ensemble increasingly fades from
view. Indeed, in the desire to get behind the text and to give a theological explanation for every detail, it may even be forgotten that human
love, which is the vehicle of the supposed allegory, may itself grant a
glimpse of the divine.

Origen's exegesis of 1.2 is characteristic (Winling 1983: 24-25). In this
verse, the woman, identified with the church, longs for the kisses of her
lover, Christ. His kisses have, in the past, been mediated by Moses and
the prophets. Now, however, she pleads for the kisses of his mouth, that

1.   For a detailed examination of this early Christian literature, see Pelletier 1989.

is, to enter into direct communication with him. Seeing him approach, she addresses him directly, praising his breasts more than wine and likening the scent of his perfumes to the richest of spices (Song 1.2). In turn he quotes Ps. 45.8 in praise of her, 'You love righteousness and hate wickedness. Therefore God, your God, has anointed you with the oil of gladness above your fellows; your robes are all fragrant with myrrh and aloes and cassia.' There follows a discussion of biblical passages in which references to perfume appear (2 Cor. 2.15; Exod. 3.34; 31.3). Origen then draws conclusions which directly challenge the morality of his readers, likening those Christians who fail to spread abroad the pleasant odour of Christ to the Psalmist who complains of his suppurating wounds (Ps. 38.6).

This example amply demonstrates the scope of theological reflection opened up by allegorical exegesis. As regards a better appreciation of the Song as a unified lyrical composition it is, however, unhelpful, for the images cease to relate to each other as imaginative elements in an organic whole but are treated individually as the occasion for reflection.

The imagery of the Song has often been related to that of certain prophetic texts (Hos. 1–3; Isa. 50.1; 54.4-8; Jer. 2–3; Ezek. 16.23) in which Israel is depicted as an unfaithful bride, yearned for and sought after by her divine lover. The prophetic texts thereby become the key to understanding the Song, for the acknowledged protagonists in the prophetic texts, Yahweh and Israel, are identified with the anonymous lovers of the Song and consequently encourage the reader to consider the Song as an allegory. The allegorical nature of the nuptial imagery as used by the prophets is itself debatable, as Stienstra (1993) has rightly pointed out, for the nuptial imagery which clusters around the notion of Yahweh as the husband of his people is, strictly speaking, better described as metaphor than as allegory. Moreover, the treatment of the imagery is radically different in so far as the prophetic texts use nuptial imagery in order to illustrate the content of covenant theology, itself a metaphor for Israel's salvation history. Allusion to this theology is however entirely absent from the Song, which is, in this respect, closer to Wisdom literature.

Indeed the imagery itself is also subtly different, for if the language of the prophets is dominated by the terminology which surrounds marriage as a legal institution, with abundant reference to betrothal, dowry, marriage, adultery and divorce, the lovers of the Song are remarkably free of the institution. Indeed the diversity of themes and motifs make it quite impossible to situate the lovers either in the context of marriage or betrothal; the element of secrecy in the refrain, 'Turn my love, be like a gazelle or a young stag' (2.17; 8.14) and the fact that the woman is subject to the authority of her brothers in 1.6-7 make it unlikely that the lovers are married. On the other hand, hints of the consummation of the relationship (5.1; 6.3) would seem to preclude betrothal. Nor are the hopes of marriage ever alluded to. If the prophets use the marriage metaphor to speak of divine fidelity in the context of human wayward-ness, the Song simply sings of love. The texts therefore are not com-parable, for in the prophets love language is subordinate to the institution, whereas in the Song it asserts love's force.

A final difference is to be noted, namely the place of fertility in both sets of texts, for if there is no mention of fertility or prosperity anywhere in the Song, except negatively as regards prosperity in 8.7, the prophets develop the theme of fertility in the context of the nuptial allegory. They do so for two reasons, firstly because it is a necessary component to marriage, and secondly because these texts arise out of the conflict with foreign fertility cults. Not only is this polemic completely foreign to the Song, but those female attributes most associated with fertility, breasts and vulva, are always described in strictly erotic terms.

Typological and *parabolic* readings of the Song constitute a variation upon the traditional allegorical interpretation. Typology (see for example Delitzsch 1875) interprets the Song in the light of the New Testament and so imposes upon the Song an interpretation which does not emerge from the text itself. Parable (see for example Buzy 1951) has the advan-tage over allegory of treating the imagery globally, therefore enabling a greater appreciation of the lyrical qualities of the Song. The identification of the main characters with Yahweh and Israel, however, finds no justification in the text. Once more theology determines our reading of Scripture, rather than allowing Scripture first to speak for itself. Indeed a similar criticism will be made of the majority of interpretations, in so far as each in some way seeks to impose upon the Song an interpretation based largely on external factors.

The *cultic interpretation* too, in its own way, has taken an interest in the imagery, with particular regard for the clues which the images might yield as to traces of liturgical use or of cultic context. Towards the end of the nineteenth century a number of these interpretations were advanced, each of which was stimulated by the translation of hitherto unknown Mesopotamian, Egyptian and Canaanite texts. Erbt (1906) suggested that the Song consisted of paschal poems of Canaanite origin, while De Jassy (1914) argued that it was a Hebrew translation of Egyptian Osiris litanies. Meek (1924) related the Song to the Tammuz cult and Wittekindt (1926) to a liturgy celebrated in Jerusalem concerning the marriage of the gods Ishtar and Tammuz. Schmökel (1956) discerned traces of a sacred marriage liturgy which had been deliberately suppressed, and Kramer (1969) proposed that the Song accompanied a form of sacred marriage rite persistent in Solomonic times. Finally Pope (1977: 210-29) argued that the language of the Song indicates its early origins and that the background is the love feast accompanying the funerary rite.

Of the many difficulties presented by these interpretations, most pertinent to our study is the way in which certain isolated images are deemed to allude to divine personages or mythological scenes. Meek, for example, claims that the watchmen of 3.3 and 5.7 remind us of the gatekeepers Ishtar has to pass on her journey to the netherworld (1956: 118) and argues that the allusion in 4.8 is to Astarte who descends each year from the mountains of Lebanon to the Adonis river at Aphaca (1956: 123). Likewise, the theophanic language of 6.10 is not an example of poetic hyperbole, underlining the unique beauty of the woman, but rather an indication that the she is divine (1956: 133). According to this kind of exegesis, images which should be regarded as part of a cohesive imaginative fabric are made to bear the weight of the interpretation of the Song as a whole, and this on the basis of the most slender evidence.[2] Moreover the identification of the lovers of the Song with divine personages and their actions with sacred actions approaches traditional allegory. The images thereby cease to engage with each other as elements constitutive of an imaginative whole. Instead they begin to operate at different levels, a process which distracts from their lyrical purpose.

The *dramatic theory* suggests that the Song is a play to be performed. The antiquity of the interpretation[3] was a great source of stimulus to nineteenth-century proponents of the dramatic theory, yet it was in vain that they strove to agree upon the number of main characters and their

2.　Even more pertinent in this respect is the interpretation of Pope which hinges principally on two texts, 2.4-5 and 8.6.

3.　The Codex Alexandrinus and Codex Sinaiticus offer notes in the margin, assigning parts to speakers. In line with this tradition, Origen describes the Song as a nuptial poem in dramatic form in the first lines of his prologue (Winling 1983: 23-24).

relationship with each other. Particularly contentious was the role of Solomon in the Song, considered by some to be a villain (Ewald 1826; Renan 1860) and by Delitzsch (1875) to be a hero.

The Song does not, however, place Solomon in the foreground, either as hero or villain, as the story-lines proposed by the above-mentioned critics suggest. Nor is there sufficient consistency of character, setting and tone to maintain any clear narrative line. Rather, the story of the Song lies in the shifting emotions of the lovers' hearts as disclosed by the sequence of images therein. The epithets by which they address each other do not therefore refer to external reality, but rather to the reality of the heart. Thus it is that the lovers are many things to each other simultaneously, brother and sister, bride, king, dove. Once again the imagery of the Song must reclaim its poetic potency as an imaginative ensemble, for like the cultic reading, the dramatic theory isolates particular images in order to substantiate a general interpretation of the Song.

The aim of this study now comes more clearly into focus; by contrast with allegorical and cultic readings, I shall not try to get behind the text in order to interpret the imagery in the light of a general theory. Instead, I aim to explore the way in which the images operate throughout the poem as metaphors for love. By contrast with dramatic theories, on the other hand, the emphasis will not be upon what the lovers do but rather what they feel. The poet expresses this in the multiplicity of images by means of which the lovers address each other. These images and their relationship to each other are the subject of this book.

When we begin to look at the imagery of the Song, we are immediately struck by its disconcerting nature. It should be recognized, however, that if certain images seem extraordinary to us it is surely because they belong to an age and culture so different from our own, a culture with its own set of references, its own ideal of beauty and so on. A different culture may also draw upon a different set of commonplaces in the elaboration of its imagery, hence the need to pay close attention to indications elsewhere in the Old Testament as to what these particular associations might be. Keel, in his iconographic commentary (1986), has disclosed the depth of resonance of certain images of the Song in the wider culture of the ancient Near East and particularly in Egypt. We should not however be too daunted by this breadth of reference, for it is also the genius of the poet to combine literary commonplaces in a surprising and innovative way.

Keeping these remarks in mind, let us take a closer look at specific images:

> Your neck is like David's tower,
> built in encircling courses,
> a thousand shields hang upon it,
> all of them the shields of warriors.

Segal (1962) speaks of the playfulness of such descriptions of the loved one. The Song, he says, 'abounds in playfulness, in gentle raillery'. Indeed, according to Segal, the otherwise grotesque comparisons of 4.4 quoted above can be rationally explained only as playful banter.

Soulen (1967), on the other hand, understands this same imagery to be primarily the expression of the poet's joy, the outpouring of emotion aroused by the loved one. According to him, this kind of imagery is not primarily representational but presentational, the purpose being to translate the lover's feelings and sense experiences into art.

On the basis of these two very different ways of defining the function of the Song's imagery, a debate henceforth opens up as regards the extent to which the objective correlate of the imagery is important to its interpretation. Pope (1977), for example, finds justification in the otherwise exaggerated comparisons of 4.4 and 7.4, 5 for a mythological interpretation. In so doing he implicitly sides with Segal, for his argument is based upon the impossibility of such descriptions as realistic portrayals of the loved one. Of 4.4, he writes, 'The size of the damsel's neck stretches poetic hyperbole a bit as applied to a peasant lass or any earthly creature...If the lady is divine, her proportions would not be abnormal'. Müller (1984) also tends in this direction. For him the high degree of metaphoric distance as regards certain images contributes to the magical or aesthetic effect of the imagery.

What then is to be said about the interpretation of the imagery?

For Soulen it is surely the evocative capacity of language which is supremely important. This relates to the power of the imagination to give voice to realms of experience too deep for words, to order and give meaning to our sensations and intuitions. It is well to remember, however, the basic rule of metaphor, that if particular images are to work, they require to be concrete, for the poetic image is necessarily 'a figure of speech which expresses some similarity or analogy' (Watson 1984: 251). The image therefore must have some connection, objective or emotional, with its referent.

Segal, on the other hand, is perplexed by the element of surprise evident in the Song's imagery, yet a second basic tenet of metaphor is that the image is dependent for its effectiveness on the tension 'between thoughts of different things active together' (Richards 1936: 93). The surprising nature of the Song's imagery is therefore entirely to be expected. Indeed, an element of surprise is essential to the success of the imagery.

Fox (1985) displays a more balanced approach to the Song's imagery. In his analysis of the problem, he insists upon the objective feature that each image has in common with its referent, making that particular image, rather than any other, uniquely appropriate. He makes particular reference to the descriptive songs, studied by Segal and Soulen, in which each part of the body in turn is the subject of detailed description. According to him, the very form of these *wasfs* encourages the reader to expect some correspondence between image and referent:

> The poet does not merely heap up lovely images (or images of lovely things) to overwhelm us with imagined sense-impressions, but rather seeks a particular image for each part of the body and organises these images in an itemised list. The one-to-one correspondences between image and parts of the body make us feel that some quality peculiar to each part, and not just a general feeling of affection, calls forth these images (Fox 1985: 275).

Fox also recognizes that this objective sensory resemblance alone does not explain the effectiveness of the imagery, but that this resemblance is necessary to make the metaphor possible. The emotional impact of the imagery of which Soulen spoke comes not from this common ground but from the metaphoric distance which is created when two very different objects are juxtaposed, a scarlet thread and the woman's lips (4.3), for example.

Finally, as Richards (1936) has rightly pointed out, there is a wealth of nuance in imaginative expression. Image and referent may be more or less prominent, and the ground of the metaphor may be more or less clear. If, on occasions, we are unable to discern the analogy, that does not mean that it does not exist or that the metaphor has failed. Rather, it encourages the reader to sharpen his or her appetite, to attend more closely to the images in question.

The importance of considering each image in the context of an imaginative ensemble cannot be overemphasized. This is particularly true of the Song in which the images are an important element in the constitution of its unity, a unity much contested in the history of the Song's exegesis. Those who do hold this view justify themselves variously: structural and rhetorical studies (Angénieux 1968, Shea 1980 and Exum 1973) have drawn attention to the contribution of stylistic devices such as chiasmus, paronomasia and repetition to the creation of a unified ensemble.

Against this background, Elliott (1989), Fox (1985) and Murphy (1990) emphasize the importance of 'poetic structure and content working together' for they consider it a weakness on the part of structural studies that they are so concerned with establishing objective criteria for poetic divisions that little regard is paid to content. Elliott in particular makes it her aim to account for the organic unity of the Song. She does so by arguing on the one hand for a six-part macro-structure on the basis of refrains which, though well integrated, constitute poetic divisions and act as hinges between parts. She also however draws attention to correspondences between units, particularly at the level of shared vocabulary.

It is only with Grober (1984), however, that we find an attempt to account for the unity of the Song solely on the basis of its imagery. Grober demonstrates the interrelatedness of the Song's imagery by reference to the metaphor 'his lips are lotuses dripping with liquid myrrh', the passage of whose constituent parts he charts throughout the Song. My task is to continue his work as regards the many other motifs which recur there.

In the course of this study we will soon discover that, on the whole, the images belong to three well-defined milieux, the court, the family and nature, within which smaller units of imagery may be discerned. Each of these is made up of images which are sufficiently closely related to each other to constitute an *imaginative field*. Courtly imagery, itself a broad imaginative field, comprises several such fields, some of which are related more closely than others to the predominant milieu. There is the imaginative field of kingship, for example, which is related more closely to the court than the imagery of war, which radiates from the latter. Some fields are based upon objects, the imagery of adornment, the imagery of flora and fauna for example; others are based upon relationships, sibling relationships or parent–child relationships for example; yet others are constituted by social position, the daughters of Jerusalem or regal imagery, for example. The titles of the sections within chs. 1–3 correspond to these imaginative fields whose interaction we will observe in the course of the study.

The coining of the term 'imaginative field' was stimulated largely in response to the work of Stienstra (1993), who alerts us to the importance of locating individual metaphors in a metaphorical system rather than treating them in isolation. She bases her work on that of Kittay and Lehrer (1981), who argue that the basic unit of metaphor is in fact the semantic field rather than the word or even the sentence. For Stienstra, therein lies the key to unravelling the complex network of imagery relating to divorce, adultery, jealousy and so on in the Old Testament, each instance of which in some way refers to the metaphorical concept that Yahweh is the husband of his people.

As regards the Song, no single metaphorical concept may be said to organize the imagery to be found therein. The basic insight of the importance of setting individual images in the context of related imagery is however an extremely useful one. It is the stimulus to my attempt to observe how these ranges of related images work together. Can we discern in their movement, for example, any narrative dimension? Secondly, what are the consequences of the interaction of imaginative fields? That is, what are the depths of metaphorical density which this repetitive dimension opens up? Finally, on the basis of my analysis, may we draw any conclusions concerning the important questions of authorship and interpretation which I have left aside in the meantime?

I begin my study with a translation of the text of the Song and a discussion of the meaning of difficult words and phrases and of textual cruxes. The translation does not aim to be authoritative, but is intended both to mirror and to test the conclusions of the study. The headings are purely functional, identifying the broad changes of scene and speaker, and should not be taken as implying adherence to any theory of the Song's provenance or structure. Indeed, one of my main concerns is to eschew such theories, which are nearly always dependent on factors outside the Song.

TRANSLATION

1.1	Prologue	The Song of Songs by Solomon.

1.2	Woman	O that he would kiss me,
		with the kisses of his mouth,
		for your embrace is better than wine,
1.3		the fragrance of your oils is pleasing,
		your presence, streaming[1] perfume;
		that is why the maidens love you.
1.4		Draw me after you! Let us run!
		Let the king bring me[2] to his chambers!
		In you we will rejoice and be glad,
		we will praise your embrace more than wine.
		How right they are to love you!

1.5		Black am I, yet beautiful, O daughters of Jerusalem,
		like the tents of Kedar,
		like the curtains of Solomon.
1.6		Do not stare at me because I am dark,
		because the sun has scorched me.
		My mother's sons were angry with me
		and sent me to watch over the vineyards;
		my own vineyard I did not tend!

1.7		Tell me, my true love,
		where you graze your flock,
		where you rest at noon,
		for why should I go about like a harlot
		among the flocks of your companions?

1.   *tûraq* is the third person feminine singular *hophal* imperfect of the root *ryq*, 'to pour out', hence the translation 'streaming'. The difficulty is that the feminine verbal form does not agree with the masculine noun *šemen*, 'oil'. Gordis (1974: 78), however, points out that a number of nouns are ambivalent in gender.

2.   *maškenî* is translated by S and Symmachus as if it were an imperative, 'bring me'. One is thereby obliged to change the pronominal suffix of *ḥadarâw* from 'his' to 'your chambers'. The verb is more easily translated as a second person masculine singular *hiphil* perfect, 'he brought me', or as a precative perfect, 'Let the king bring me!' (cf. Job 31.35). Read as a precative perfect (Gibson 1994: 69) the form corresponds to the jussive of 1.2, 'O that he would kiss me!'

1.8	Man	If you do not know, O fairest of women,
		go, follow the tracks of the sheep
		and pasture your kids
		by the shepherd's tents.

1.9   To a mare[3] of Pharaoh's chariotry[4]
            I compare you, my love:
1.10   your cheeks, lovely between earrings,
            your neck, through beaded collar.
1.11   We shall make for you, earrings of gold,
            set with spangles of silver.

1.12   Woman   While the king lies on his couch,
               my nard gives forth its fragrance.
1.13   My beloved is to me a sachet of myrrh,
               between my breasts he takes his rest;
1.14   my beloved is to me a spray of henna blossom,
               in the vineyards of Ein-Gedi.

1.15   Man   How beautiful you are, my love,
               ah, how beautiful,
               your eyes like doves!

1.16   Woman   How beautiful you are, my love,
               and how handsome!
               Our couch is greened over;
1.17   the beams of our house, cedar,
               are rafters, all of pine.

2.1   I am a flower of Sharon,
               a water-lily growing in the valleys.

2.2   Man   Like a lily among thorns,
               is my love among maidens.

2.3   Woman   Like an apple tree among the trees of the forest,

---

3.   *susatî* is characterized by an old genitive ending, the *hireq compaginis* (Joüon 1947: 222, fig. 93b). The archaic ending was possibly chosen so as to rhyme with the term of endearment *ra'yatî*.

4.   *rikbê* is the masculine plural construct of *rekeb*, a 'chariot', a noun most often used in the singular to denote a collective plural. It has therefore been asked how one mare could link up with several chariots? It seems likely that the answer lies in those plurals of generalization which are characteristic of the Song (1.4, 12, 17; 2.9; 3.1) (Joüon 1947: 418, fig. 136j). The form is used to underline the woman's incomparability.

is my beloved among young men.
With great delight I sat in his shade
and his fruit was sweet to my taste.

2.4   To the banqueting hall[5] he led me
and his banner over me is love.

2.5   Sustain me with raisin cakes,
revive me with apples,
for I am sick with love.

2.6   His left hand holds my head
and his right hand is round me!

2.7   I charge you, daughters of Jerusalem,
by the gazelles and hinds of the field;
do not arouse or awaken love
until it is ready.

2.8   The sound of my beloved! Here he comes,
bounding over the mountains,
leaping over the hills.

2.9   My beloved is like a gazelle
or a young stag.
There he stands behind our wall,
peering in at the windows,
gazing through the lattice.

2.10   My beloved spoke, saying to me;
(Man)   'Arise, my love
my fair one, come away.

2.11   for see, the winter is past,
the rains are over and gone;

2.12   the vines appear on the earth,

---

5.   Found nowhere else in the Old Testament, *bêt hayyâyîn* is probably a shortened form of the *bêt mištte hayyâyîn* of Est. 7.8 where it describes King Ahasuerus's banqueting hall. Not all the references to the *bêt mištte hayyâyîn* are located in a regal setting however. In Eccl. 7.2 and Jer. 16.8 the setting is not specified, leaving open taverns and wedding festivities to be the likely context. Indeed in the light of the reference to 'the voice of the bridegroom' and 'the voice of the bride' which follow immediately thereafter in Jer. 16.9, it would seem likely that the place of feasting referred to is the place where wedding celebrations were held. References such as these have encouraged critics to identify the 'house of wine' with banqueting hall or tavern, depending on their view of the Song's overall function. A third option, proposed by Pope (1977: 210-29) is that it is a place of sacral celebration in the context of funerary rites. In the light of the imagery of 2.4, the translation proposed here accords with a regal setting without wishing thereby to imply any particular provenance for the Song. The image is hyperbolic, comparable to the woman's declaration a few verses later that she is 'sick with love' (2.5c).

the season of birdsong[6] is come
and the coo of the turtledove
is heard in our land.

2.13   The fig tree sees its green fruits ripen
and the vines are in blossom and full of fragrance.
Arise, my love,
my fair one, come away.

2.14   My dove, hidden in the crannies of the rock,
in the secret places of the mountain steep,[7]
let me see your face,
let me hear your voice;
for your voice is sweet,
your face is lovely.'

2.15   Woman   Catch us the jackals, the little jackals
that despoil the vineyards,
for our vineyards are in bloom.

2.16   My beloved is mine and I am his,
he grazes among the water-lilies.

2.17   Until the day breathes
and the shadows flee,
Turn, my beloved, and flee like
a gazelle or a young stag
on the mountains of Bether.

3.1   Night after night on my bed
I sought my true love,
I sought him, but did not find him.

3.2   I said, 'I will arise now and go the rounds of the city
through the streets and squares,
seeking my true love'.
I sought him but could not find him.

3.3   The watchmen found me
as they made their rounds of the city.

---

6.   *hazzamîr*, a *hapax legomenon*, is associated with two different roots, *zmr*, meaning 'to cut'
or 'to sing'. The reader is thereby both referred back to the mention of the appearance of blossom
(2.12a) and forward to the mention of birdsong (2.12c). The fact that the Gezer Calendar places the
time for pruning much later (around July–August) is not the primary concern of the poet. His or her
desire is to express by means of stylistic economy the rapidity of the changing seasons and the
urgency with which the woman is summoned.

7.   *hammadregâ* is found elsewhere only in Ezek. 38.20. There, the plural form parallels a
reference to mountains and walls. The image is one of inaccessibility.

'Have you seen my true love?'

3.4   Scarcely had I passed them
when I found my true love,
I held him, now I will not let him go
till I bring him to my mother's house,
to the chamber of her who conceived me.

3.5   I charge you, daughters of Jerusalem,
by the hinds and gazelles of the field;
Do not rouse or awaken love
until it is ready.

3.6	Daughters of Jerusalem	Who is this coming up from the wilderness like a column of smoke, perfumed with myrrh and frankincense, with all kinds of merchant's powers?
3.7	Narrator	Look! It is the litter of Solomon; sixty warriors escort it, of the warriors of Israel,
3.8		all of them girt with swords, all of them expert in war each with his sword at his side against the terrors of the night.
3.9		The King made a palanquin for himself, Solomon made it out of wood from Lebanon.
3.10		Its posts he made of silver, its roof of gold, Its seat of purple, its interior lovingly wrought.[8]
3.10e-11		Daughters of Jerusalem, go forth![9] Look, daughters of Zion! upon Solomon the king in the crown with which his mother crowned him on the day of his wedding, the day of his gladness and joy.
4.1	Man	How beautiful you are, my love, how beautiful! Your eyes are doves

---

8.   Several emendations have been proposed as regards the adverbial accusative *'ahabâ*, 'with love' (Pope 1977: 446). These however do not add anything to the MT.

9.   MT implies that the daughters of Jerusalem are responsible for the decoration of the interior. Most modern commentators (Keel, Pope, Murphy, Fox) agree that it makes more sense to link the daughters of Jerusalem (3.10e) to the daughters of Zion (3.11a). Both are addressed in the vocative. The *mem* of *mibbᵉnôt* should be treated as enclitic, belonging to the preceding *'ahabâ(m)* (3.10e).

behind your veil,
Your hair like a flock of goats,
moving down Mount Gilead.

4.2   Your teeth are like a flock of shorn ewes,
freshly come up from the washing,
all of them have twins,
none has lost a lamb.

4.3   Your lips are like a scarlet thread
and your mouth,[10] lovely.
Your cheeks, like halves of a pomegranate
behind your veil.

4.4   Your neck is like David's tower
built in encircling courses;
a thousand shields hang upon it,
all of them the shields of warriors.

4.5   Your two breasts are like two fawns,
twin fawns of a gazelle
grazing among the water-lilies.

4.6   Until the day breathes
and the shadows flee,
I shall take myself to the mountain of myrrh
and to the hill of frankincense.

4.7   You are all fair my love,
fair without a flaw.

4.8   <Come>[11] with me from Lebanon, my bride,
with me from Lebanon, come!
Hurry down from the heights of Amana,
from the summits of Senir and Hermon,
from the lion's lairs
and the hills where panthers prowl.

4.9   You have ravished my heart, my sister, my bride,

10.   *ûmidbarêk* is translated by 'mouth' rather than by 'speech' (cf. LXX and Vg) on the grounds of parallelism; the description deals with parts of the body, hence the organ of speech is more appropriate than the act of speaking.

11.   *'ittî* is revocalized by LXX, S and Vg to read *'ettî*, the feminine singular *qal* imperative of the verb *'th*, 'to come'. Read thus, the assumption is that he calls her to come *to* him. The emphasis of the MT is slightly different, he calls her to accompany him as he descends the mountainside. For the sake of fluency, the form is translated here by 'Come!'

you have stolen it,
with just one of your glances,[12]
with one jewel of your necklace.

4.10 How fair is your love, my sister, my bride;
your love is better than wine,
your perfumes more fragrant than any spice.

4.11 Your lips drop sweetness like the honeycomb,
my bride,
honey and milk are under your tongue,
and your dress has the scent of Lebanon.

4.12 A garden locked is my sister,
my bride,
a garden locked, a fountain sealed;

4.13 your shoots are an orchard of pomegranates,
full of choice fruits,

4.14 of spikenard and saffron,
aromatic cane and cinnamon,
every kind of frankincense tree,
myrrh and aloes,
indeed every exquisite spice—

4.15 a garden fountain, a spring of living water,
streaming[13] from Lebanon.

4.16 Woman Awake, north wind, and come, south wind!
Blow upon my garden,
let its fragrance be spread abroad,
that my beloved may come to his garden
and eat its most choice fruit.

5.1 Man I have come to my garden, my sister and bride
I have gathered my myrrh and my spices,

---

12. The disparity between the masculine numeral 'one' and the feminine plural 'eyes' has caused some difficulty. According to Ginsburg (1970) however, parts of the body which are usually feminine do sometimes appear in the masculine (cf. Job 31.20; Zech. 4.10). According to Gordis (1974: 55), it is an Aramaic construction.

13. The third image in the sequence depends upon the 'living waters' of the second, for $noz^e lîm$ is a verbal form, a plural participle, preceded by a simple *waw*. The provenance of these streaming waters however is no longer a single well but the hollows of the Lebanese hillside (4.15b), hence the inclination to translate the participle by a noun 'streams'. In favour of this rendering is the parallelism in Ps. 78.44 of $y^e 'orêhem$ and $noz^e lêhem$. In this translation, however, the tenuous link with the 'well of living waters' is retained in order to convey the way in which one element fuses with and grows out of another. The form is highly onomatopoeic, conveying by means of the combination of its sounds, the energetic movement of the cool, clear waters.

I have eaten my honeycomb and my honey,
and drink my wine and my milk.

Eat friends, and drink,
till you are drunk with love!

5.2   Woman   I slept, but my heart was awake.
Listen! My beloved is knocking
'Open to me,
my sister, my love,
my dove, my perfect one,
for my heart is drenched with dew,
my locks with the damp of the night'.

5.3   'I had put off my robe,
how could I put it on again?
I had bathed my feet,
how could I dirty them?'

5.4   My beloved thrust his hand in through
the keyhole
and my heart turned over when he spoke.[14]

5.5   I arose to open to my love
and my hands dripped with myrrh,
my fingers ran with liquid myrrh
upon the handles of the latch.

5.6   I opened to my love,
but my love had turned and was gone.
I swooned at his flight.

I sought him, but could not find him
I called, but there was no answer.
5.7   The watchmen found me,
as they made their rounds of the city.
They beat me, they wounded me,
the guards of the walls
stripped me of my cloak.
5.8   I charge you, daughters of Jerusalem,
if you find my love,
what you should tell him is this,
that I am sick with love.

---

14.   *b^e dabb^e rô* has been displaced from 5:6 to 4:8 where it makes better sense.

5.9	Daughters of Jerusalem	What is your beloved more than any other, O fairest of women? What is your beloved more than any other, that you give us this charge?
5.10	Woman	My beloved is bright red, outstanding among ten thousand.
5.11		His head is gold, finest gold. His locks are like palm-fronds, black as a raven.
5.12		His eyes are like doves beside streams of water; bathed in milk, they sit steady, the river in spate.
5.13		His cheeks are like beds of spices yielding[15] fragrance, his lips are water-lilies, they drop liquid myrrh.
5.14		His arms are rods of gold, encrusted with jewels, his stomach is a bar of ivory, adorned with lapis lazuli.
5.15		His legs are marble pillars, set on bases of finest gold; his bearing is like Lebanon, noble as the cedar.
5.16		His mouth is sheer sweetness, wholly desirable. Such is my beloved, such is my love, O daughters of Jerusalem.
6.1	Daughters of Jerusalem	Where has your beloved gone, O fairest of women? Which way did your beloved turn that we may seek him with you?
6.2	Woman	My beloved has gone down to his garden to the beds of spices,

15. *migdᵉlôt*, 'towers', has been revocalized to correspond to the feminine plural *piel* participle *mᵉgaddᵉlôt* from the root *gdl*, 'to put forth', 'to yield', 'to grow' (*piel*). The revocalized reading enhances the parallelism with 5.13d.

to graze in the gardens
and to pick the water-lilies.

6.3   I am my beloved's and my beloved is mine;
he grazes his flock among the water-lilies.

6.4   Man   You are beautiful as Tirzah, my love
and lovely as Jerusalem,
awesome as an army with banners.

6.5   Turn your eyes away from me;
they dazzle me.
Your hair is like a flock of goats
moving down Mount Gilead;
6.6   Your teeth are like a flock of shorn ewes,
freshly come up from the washing,
all of them have twins,
none has lost a lamb.
6.7   Your cheeks are like halves of a pomegranate,
behind your veil.

6.8   There may be sixty queens and eighty concubines
and innumerable young women,
6.9   but one alone is my dove, my perfect one,
her mother's only one,
the favourite of her who bore her.
Maidens see her and call her blessed,
queens and concubines also, and they praise her.
6.10   Who is this that looks forth as the dawn,
lovely as the moon, radiant as the sun,
awesome as an army with banners?

6.11   Man   I made off down to the nut orchard
to see the new growth in the valleys,
to see if the vines had budded
or if the pomegranates were in flower.
6.12   Before I knew it, she set me
among the chariots of my people, as prince![16]

---

16.   *napšî* is understood to be the subject of *yadaʿtî*. Secondly, the *maqqeph* is probably the result of dittography, the final *yod* of *ʿammî* having been reduplicated by a similar form. The noun therefore stands in apposition, not to the preceding word (cf. Robert, Tournay and Feuillet 1963: 234) but to the preceding phrase. Read thus, the verse makes good sense. It describes the way in which the woman makes her lover feel like a prince, someone marked for all kinds of privileges. He

| 7.1 | Male Chorus | Come back, come back, O Shulamite |
| | | come back, come back, that we may gaze on you. |

| | Man | Why do you gaze upon the Shulamite[17] |
| | | as upon a dancer before the camps![18] |

7.2   How graceful are your sandalled feet,
O prince's daughter!
The curves of your thighs are like ornaments,
the work of a skilled hand.

7.3   Your navel is a rounded bowl,
may it never lack spiced wine.
Your belly is a heap of wheat,
encircled by water-lilies.

7.4   Your two breasts are like two fawns,
twin fawns of a gazelle.

7.5   Your neck is like an ivory tower.
Your eyes are pools in Heshbon
beside the gate of Bath-rabbim.
Your nose is like a tower of Lebanon,
looking towards Damascus.

7.6   Your head crowns you like Carmel
your flowing locks have the sheen of purple;
a king is caught in their movement.

---

is simply overwhelmed as he strolls in the orchard. For a discussion of the verse, see Gordis 1974: 95; Pope 1977: 565; Gerleman 1965: 191; Fox 1985: 53.

17. The epithet *haššulamît*, from the root *šlm*, bears within it a number of possibilities. It reminds the reader of Solomon, the king who is sometimes associated with the lovers (1.5; 3.7, 11), of Jerusalem, the city to which the woman's confidantes belong (1.5; 2.7; 3.5; 5.8 etc.), of the perfection he attributes to her (4.2; 6.6, 9) and of the peace which he finds in her eyes (8.10). The epithet plays on all these associations at once, acting as a trigger to the imagination. The title has for this reason been left as it stands.

18. Following Gerleman (1965: 192-93) and Fox (1985: 158), *kim^ehollelet*, emended from *kimholat* (MT), is translated by 'as upon a dancer'. The feminine singular *polel* participle accompanies the unusual form *hammahanayîm*, probably the assimilation of the less usual plural form *mahanîm* (Num. 13.19), 'camps', to the place name *Mahanayîm* (2 Sam. 17.24). The presence of the definite article indicates that the intention of the poet was not primarily topographical. LXX, S and Vg all translate the form by 'camps'. In the light of this military association and the custom of women to dance before their warriors (Exod. 15.20; Judg. 11.34; 1 Sam. 18.6-7 etc.), the imagery of 7.2 begins to make sense. It relates to the appeal made to the woman in 7.1 to which her lover responds, challenging an anonymous male chorus with the propriety of their conduct; it is not that they should cease to look upon women who dance publicly in celebration of military victory (Jepthah's daughter in Judg. 11.34 or Miriam in Exod. 15.20), but that the same attention is inappropriate when it concerns a woman who is not fulfilling this public role. The Shulamite is primarily his beloved (cf. 6.4) and consequently for his eyes alone.

7.7		How beautiful, how lovely you are,
		dear one, daughter of delights![19]
7.8		There you are, stately as a palm tree,
		your breasts like its clusters.
7.9		I said, 'let me climb the palm
		and grasp its fronds'.
		Oh, may your breasts be like clusters of the vine,
		your breath sweet-scented like apples,
7.10a		and your kisses[20] like the best wine
7.10b	Woman	flowing[21] smoothly to my beloved,
7.10c	Man	passing over my lips and teeth.[22]
7.11	Woman	I am my beloved's, for me he longs;
7.12		come, my beloved, let us go out into the fields
		and lodge in the villages.
7.13		Let us go early to the vineyards
		to see if the vines have budded
		and their blossom opened,
		and if the pomegranates are in flower.
		There I shall give you my love,
7.14		when the mandrakes are full of fragrance,
		and all choice fruits are over our door,
		fruits new and old,
		which I have in store for you, my love.
8.1		If only you were a brother to me,
		nursed at my mother's breast.
		Then if I met you outside, I could
		kiss you,
		and no-one would despise me.
8.2		I should lead you to my mother's house,

19.   *batan'ûgîm*, 'with delights', makes better sense if it is recognized that haplography has taken place. The scribe has most likely omitted a *taw* after the initial *beth*. The *beth* therefore has become an inseparable preposition. Rather than one word, two words should be in evidence, *bat ta'anûgîm*, 'daughter of delights'.

20.   *hôlek*, literally 'palate', but more precisely the woman's kisses which are compared to the best wine (cf. 1.2, 4.10).

21.   *dôbeb*, a *hapax legomenon* probably derived from the Aramaen *d(w)b*, 'to flow', rather than *dbb*, 'to murmur' (cf. Pope 1977: 640).

22.   *śiptê yᵉšenîm* has been emended to *śiptê wᵉšenay* by LXX, S and Vg who also read the final *mem* as enclitic, 'my lips and teeth'. It is the sense of reciprocity conveyed by the shift in speakers that is important.

and bring you to her
who conceived me;[23]
I should give you spiced wine to drink
and the juice of my pomegranates.

8.3   His left hand holds my head
and his right hand is round me!

8.4   I charge you, daughters of Jerusalem,
Would you arouse or stir up love,
before it is ready?

8.5   Daughters of   Who is this coming up from the wilderness,
        Jerusalem   leaning on her beloved?

        Woman   Under the apple tree I woke you,
There your mother was in labour with you,
there she who bore you, laboured.

8.6   Set me as a seal upon your heart,
as a seal upon your arm,
for love is strong as death,
jealousy, relentless as the grave,
its shafts, shafts of fire,
more furious than any flame.[24]

8.7   Mighty waters cannot quench love,
no river can sweep it away;
if someone were to offer for love,
all the wealth of his house,
he would be laughed to scorn.

8.8   'We have a little sister;
she has no breasts.
What shall we do for our sister,
on the day she is spoken for?'

8.9   'If she is a wall,
we shall build upon it a silver parapet;
if she is a door,
we shall board it up with a plank of cedar.'

---

23. *tᵉlammᵉdenî* may be translated 'she will teach me' or 'you will teach me'. In line with LXX and S who emend the form to parallel 3.4, I have emended to *teldenî*, 'she who conceived me'.

24. The Ben Naphtali manuscript adds a *mappiq* to the final *he* of *šalhebetyâ*, thereby making explicit a possible allusion to the divine name. The form however has simply been translated by the superlative as is the custom in the Old Testament (Prov. 1.12; Isa. 5.14; Hab. 2.5). LXX and Vg understand the final *he* to be the third person feminine singular pronominal suffix referring to the noun *'ahabâ*.

8.10   I am a wall, and my breasts are like towers;
                so in his eyes, I am one who brings peace.

8.11   Solomon has a vineyard at Baal-Hamon;
                he has given the vineyard over to keepers;
                each is to bring for its fruit
                a thousand pieces of silver.
8.12   The vineyard before me is mine,
                my very own,
                keep your thousand pieces, O Solomon,
                give those who guard its fruit, their two hundred.

8.13   Man   While you linger in the gardens
                my friends are waiting for your voice.
                Let me hear it too.

8.14   Woman   Quick, my love
                be like a gazelle
                or a young stag
                upon the mountains of spice.

Chapter 1

COURTLY IMAGERY

Regal Imagery

At least in the early chapters of the Song, regal imagery is particularly associated with the male lover. In 1.4, the metaphor is used by the woman as a way of expressing her awe and admiration. It also permits her to express his incomparability, which makes her assume that the maidens of 1.3 join her in his praise:

> Draw me after you! Let us run!
> Let the king bring me to his chambers!
> In you we will rejoice and be glad,
> we will praise your embrace more than wine ;
> How right they are to love you!

In 1.12, as in 1.4, the image of the king is associated with the heady fragrances which convey his presence to her:

> While the king lies on his couch,
> my nard gives forth its fragrance

Whereas in 1.4 the movement is into the intimacy of the king's chamber, in 1.12 the fragrance of the woman's nard is sufficient to transport them from the king's couch to the vineyards of Ein-Gedi:

> My beloved is to me a spray of henna blossom
> in the vineyards of Ein-Gedi.

A third image, that of 2.4, contributes to this same courtly ambience:

> To the house of wine he led me,
> and his banner[1] over me is love.

---

1. More recent commentators, Gordis (1974: 81), Pope (1977: 325-76), Falk (1982: 115), Fox (1985: 108) and Murphy (1990: 132) relate the noun *degel* to the Akkadian root *dagâlu*, 'to see' or 'look at'. The image therefore is of the man who

Although the king himself is not mentioned, the image of the banner is sufficient to evoke a regal milieu. The associations of this image are moreover extremely rich. A banner is raised to mark capture. It is also a sign of the presence of the one it represents and of identification, on the part of the flag-bearer, with him. It suggests that her lover is not only her captor but, most importantly, her king, and that he is extremely proud to be so.

Though the preceding verses, 1.15–2.3, are dominated by natural imagery, the image of the banner fits into this context quite naturally, thanks to the harmonizing of these two settings, courtly and natural, in 1.12-14 quoted above. Moreover there is an imaginative connection between 2.3 and 2.4, for the description of the woman sitting in the shade of the apple tree in 2.3 anticipates the image of the banner raised over her head in 2.4. Still more significant is the way in which the language of kingship is associated on each occasion—1.4, 1.12 and 2.4—with the lover's intimacy, evoked either in terms of scent or of food and drink. We have noted the common reference to scent in the immediate context of 1.2 and 1.12. Now we must note that 2.4 is reminiscent of the imagery of 1.4 by a common reference to feasting; if in 1.2 she claims that his love is better than wine, in 2.4 he takes her to the wine house. The image of the feast is continued in 2.5 by the desire on her part to be sustained in his absence by fresh fruits:

> Sustain me with raisin cakes,
> revive me with apples;
> for I am sick with love.

Roles are reversed in 7.6. Now, he is likened to a king who is rendered powerless by the very sight of her hair (7.6c). Consequently, he ceases to exercise his kingship and it is she instead who takes control. Thus it is that the attributes of kingship are henceforth applied to her:

looks lovingly upon his lover. Pope (1977: 376) argues that the noun *dagâlu* also designates 'intent'. In other words, he looks on her with desire. Apart from 5.10, however, on every instance in which the verb appears in the Old Testament it is specifically in a military context (Num. 1.52; 2.2-3, 10, 17-18, 25, 34; 10.18, 22, 25; Ps. 20.6). Indeed the ancient versions consistently take *degel* to mean a 'military unit'. LXX reads *tagma*, 'a unit drawn up in military order'. AV, RSV and JB translate the noun by 'ensign' or 'banner' on the grounds that the link between Akkadian root and the military unit of the versions was the banner or ensign by means of which the unit could be identified. The reference in Ps. 20.6 is to a banner—and not a military unit—that is raised.

Your head crowns you like Carmel,
and your flowing locks have the sheen of purple;
a king is caught in their movement.

Thus far, the image of kingship has been applied to the male lover as a way of conveying her admiration. 7.6, however, alerts the reader to the presence of another theme which grows in the wake of the first, namely that of the gradual ascent of the woman to a position of quasi-queenship. This development does not depend on the framework of a liturgy or drama for its meaning. It is simply implied by a shift in the balance of the images which make up the Song. The 'story' remains metaphor. The 'story' begins in 1.5.

Black am I, yet beautiful,
O daughters of Jerusalem
like the tents of Kedar,
like the curtains of Solomon.

The precise intention of the verse has been widely discussed. The debate focuses on the function of the *waw* of *wᵉna'wâ*, whether it is meant to establish a contrast between blackness and beauty (Fox 1985: 101) or whether it emphatically asserts that black is beautiful (Falk 1982: 110). Fox considers the tone to be sheepish. Falk reads it as an outburst of pride. The ambiguity persists in the relationship of the similes which follow. Interpretation varies depending on whether one considers them to be complementary or contrasting images. Fox considers the reference to loveliness in 1.5a to be parenthetical. Consequently he considers both of the images which follow (1.5cd) to describe her swarthiness.[2] Falk, on the other hand, who gives equal weight to both attributes in 1.5a, understands the similes of 1.5cd to explore ideas of blackness and loveliness in turn.

As regards the first difficulty, I have opted for 'black but beautiful', since in 1.6 she seems to be at pains to defend the swarthiness of her skin, begging the daughters of Jerusalem not to stare at her. There would be little point in explaining how she came to be dark to these city dwellers were she not ashamed of her colour. The following similes too are best considered antithetical, for the success of the parallelism of 1.5cd depends on the juxtaposition of two different ways of life, nomadic

2. Fox accepts the emendation suggested by Pope (1977: 520) that the MT *šᵉlomô* be repointed to *šalmâ*, the name of an Arabian tribe, attested in Assyrian and South Arabic sources.

(1.5c) and urban (1.5d). Together they convey her vulnerability before
the daughters of Jerusalem, who are so different from herself. The focus
of these doubts is her complexion which in 1.6 is a source of shame. In
opposition to these negative feelings, however, is a quiet confidence in
her own worth, rendering her as splendid as Solomon's curtains and as
secure as the king who dwells within (1.5d).

A search ensues and king and court give way to a pastoral scene in
1.7-8. Before it has reached its term however, her lover breaks his
silence and interrupts her search with a declaration in praise of her
beauty in 1.9-11. The image is of a mare of Pharaoh's chariotry, an
image belonging to the language of ceremonial and of war, an image
which emphasizes both her nobility and his pride:

> To a mare of Pharaoh's chariotry,
> I compare you, my love:
> your cheeks, lovely between earrings,
> your neck, through beaded collar.

The theme of the woman's redoubtability gains momentum as the
Song progresses. The first hint is given in 4.4 where her neck is
described in terms of a tower on which warriors hang their shields,
presumably a reference to her beads:[3]

> Your neck is like David's tower
> built in encircling courses;
> a thousand shields hang upon it,
> all of them the shields of warriors.

It is in ch. 6, as the Song draws to a climax, that the woman reaches a
position of pre-eminence, for she is not only associated with the royal
cities of Tirzah and Jerusalem in 6.4 but with the brilliance of the cosmos
itself:

> Who is this that looks forth as the dawn,
> lovely as the moon, radiant as the sun,
> awesome as an army with banners?

---

3.   These are a part of a necklace composed of several layers or strands. This is
the implication of the form *le talpîyôt* which Honeyman (1949: 51) relates to the
Arabic cognate *lp'*, 'to arrange in courses'. The image draws attention to the woman's
formidable inaccessibility and her awesome reserve. Although no clue is given as to
the identification of the tower, the reference to David (4.4a) is designed to strengthen
the woman's association with the Israelite monarchy.

To these regal and cosmic associations a further warlike aspect is to be added. It is evident in the final phrase 'awesome as an army with banners' and particularly in the form *nidgalôt*, whose military associations are well attested in the Old Testament.[4] Moreover the adjective *'ayummah*, 'awesome', which characterizes the woman (6.4, 10) is well suited to a military context, for apart from the Song it occurs only in Hab. 1.2, where it is used of the warring forays of the Chaldeans. There is another reason, however, why one should be reluctant to renounce the military associations of the metaphor, for deep seated in the ancient Near East is the association of love with war. Indeed it is evident in 8.6 in the description of love which sends out 'shafts of fire' (8.6e). In the background is the memory of the great love goddess, associated with fertility on the one hand and with war and pestilence on the other.[5] The woman of the Song displays none of the excesses of Anat, but she does share with her not only tenderness but also strength.[6]

The contrast with 1.6 is striking. There, she pleads with the daughters of Jerusalem not to look at her on account of the swarthiness of her skin which the sun has caused, literally by 'looking'[7] at her. Now, in 6.10, the woman is identified with the clarity and strength of the sun so as to draw their gaze. She, who was once despised and outcast, has become their queen:

> Maidens see her and call her blessed,
> queens and concubines also, and they praise her.

Subsequently, her lover does not hesitate to attribute nobility to her. In 7.1, she is associated with Solomon in the epithet *haššulamit*. In 7.2, she is hailed 'O prince's daughter'. Imagery of kingship which initially was attributed to him is more and more transferred to her as the Song progresses.

There remains the important question of the relationship of Solomon to the Song. As has often been suggested, the ascription of the Song to

4. See n. 1 above.

5. Pope (1977: 670) recalls the representation in Egyptian iconography of the love goddess standing on a horse bearing a lotus flower and a serpent in her hand. She is flanked on the one side by Rešep, the god of pestilence and war, and on the other by an ithyphallic Min.

6. Anat's warring exploits are recounted in *KTU* 1.3, ii.4-32.

7. *špz* is used elsewhere only in Job 20.9; 28.7 where it means 'to see'. Given the interchangeability of *d* and *z* in Aramaic, one can understand how *š* could be understood as meaning 'to burn' (Murphy 1990: 126).

Solomon is most likely the work of a later editor keen to associate the Song with the sapiential tradition of which Solomon was the patron, according to 1 Kgs 4.29 and the stories of 1 Kgs 3.16, 28 and 1 Kgs 10.1-10. In the Song itself, however, Solomon's position is much more ambiguous, for the historical figure has become primarily a literary motif. A survey of the references to the king will amply demonstrate this remark.

In 1.5d, the 'curtains of Solomon' constitute a positive element in the woman's assessment of her appearance. If she is dark 'like the tents of Kedar' (1.5c), she is also beautiful like the richly coloured tapestries of the king (1.5d). Solomon's standing here helps to confirm her own.

Solomon is next mentioned in 3.11. Previous to this appearance, however, is a description (3.7-10), the subject of which has proved problematic for interpreters. The problem is how 3.6 relates to 3.7. The difficulty is the interrogative pronoun *mî* which governs the feminine singular demonstrative pronoun *zō't* and the feminine singular plural participle *mᵉqutteret*. The pronoun usually refers to a person.[8] Indeed when the question is repeated in 8.5, it is to the woman that the question undoubtedly refers. The interest of the following verses however (3.7-10) is not explicitly the woman, but Solomon's litter. The woman herself is never mentioned.

Independent of this difficulty, certain traits mark out 3.7-11 from the rest of the Song. Whereas throughout the Song the lovers praise each other directly, here exceptionally the description is of something rather than of someone. Moreover 3.11 clearly refers to a wedding, the only reference to a wedding in all the Song. Finally, Solomon is the centre of attention in 3.11, contrary to the very subordinate role he plays throughout the Song. These are among the features which suggest that 3.7-11 is part of an epithalamium composed for the occasion of Solomon's wedding. The difficulty of squaring 3.6 with 3.7 may well be a clue to the limits of the insertion, for it is possible that these verses do not naturally belong together but have been made to fit on the basis of the feminine singular subject which governs both the woman in 3.6 and Solomon's litter in 3.7.[9]

The poem seems reluctant to clarify the ambiguity, however. Thus it is that a number of interpretations suggest themselves, dependent on

8.   Usually, but not exclusively, according to Joüon (1947: 446, fig. 1446).

9.   Gordis (1974: 56) takes a different view. He regards 3.6-11 as a single unit and the oldest datable unit in the Song.

whether it is the woman borne by the litter, or the litter itself, which the epithalamium describes. What is most important, however, is that the former royal wedding song is used to a precise literary end in favour of the lovers of the Song. Solomon is important in so far as his litter honours either the heroine of the Song who ascends to Jerusalem in pomp and majesty or alternatively the male lover to whom are attributed the accoutrements, including the carriage, of the king. The reference to Solomon is in both cases literary and metaphorical and in both cases also extremely positive.

The royal personage appears in less favourable perspective in 8.11-12. 8.11 begins in the formulaic style of a parable, 'Solomon had a vineyard at Baal-Hamon'.[10] The poet then describes how the vineyard was handed over to tenants who give its proprietor a proportion of the proceeds at harvest-time. Every effort is made to emphasize the high value of Solomon's vineyard in order to contrast it immediately afterwards with a particular vineyard, 'my own vineyard', which is beyond compare. The keepers who tend Solomon's vineyard also distance him from it. The speaker, by contrast, has a unique relationship with his.

The reference to 'my own vineyard' is almost certainly to be understood figuratively, for this same expression is used in 1.6e. There, the narrative suddenly becomes sharply personal and the vineyards of the Palestinian landscape focus on one particular vineyard which becomes a metaphor for the woman. The identity of the speaker is less certain. The motif of the woman's incomparability, expressed by her lover in 2.2 and 6.9, might suggest that it is he who praises her.[11] It could be, however, that the speaker is the woman and that the vineyard is an image of herself.[12] If this is indeed the case, then the images of 1.6 and 8.12

10. The song of the vineyard of Isa. 5.1-7 begins in a similar way.

11. According to Fox, the comparison is also between two very different ways of conducting a relationship; while Solomon gives his wives over to others to look after, the lover resolves to care for his vineyard himself. Falk states the same case in terms of feminism; whereas the male lover of the Song truly loves and cares for the woman he loves, Solomon regards his many wives as little more than sex objects. The place name Baal Hamon, 'lord of a multitude', accords with this interpretation.

12. Fox's argument (1985: 174) that 'only the lover can be said to possess a vineyard in the same way that Solomon does' does not reckon with the subtle shifts in perspective of which the poet has already shown himself capable. Moreover the logic of his argument does not begin to settle the question of the identity of the speaker, for it is equally likely that it is the woman who rejoices in her loved one. The

describe a radical reversal in the woman's fortunes, for she who spent her energies serving many masters in 1.6 is in 8.12 now marvellously independent.

The significance of the parable of 8.11-12 is that by means of it, the limits of metaphorical speech are laid bare. By deliberately distancing Solomon from the lovers towards the end of the Song, it becomes apparent that, in the end, the metaphor of kingship is inadequate to describe this great love. Love is not for sale, even to the most rich and powerful. The parable restates the aphorism of 8.7.

The above survey demonstrates the importance of the role of images of regality in the dialogue of the lovers. Moreover, it is evident that images of regality combine with different imaginative fields when associated with the woman and her loved one. When applied to him, images of kingship are part of the language of intimacy, blending with scents, wines and oils in the evocation of the delight of the lovers in each other's presence. When associated with the woman, however, they take on military and cosmic dimensions, expressing her lover's admiration but also underlining those qualities which make her a redoubtable partner. Not only does the language of regality engage directly with the above-mentioned imaginative fields but it draws into its sphere of influence images belonging to other related imaginative fields and becomes a focus for them. The language of wealth and splendour, for example, by means of which the lovers praise each other, is entirely consonant with this imagery. So too are the daughters of Jerusalem, representative of the courtly entourage which finds its focus in the king.

Regal images moreover shift and combine with these related imaginative constellations in such a way as to show how he becomes captive to love and how she never ceases to grow—to the point of quasi-cosmic status—in his estimation. Therein lies the narrative function of the regal imagery, telling as it does a 'story' which nevertheless remains metaphor. Solomon is integrated into this metaphorical system only to denounce it at the last minute and thereby lay bare the limits of language to speak about love. The narrative dimension of the imagery is extremely important to the dynamic of the Song, just as the capacity of the imagery to become a natural focus of courtly imagery is important to its imaginative coherence. These two factors together mean that regal imagery occupies a preeminent position among the courtly images.

image of the vineyard may just as readily be a symbol of the male lover as of the woman, for has she not already eaten of 'his fruit' (2.4)?

The Daughters of Jerusalem

The daughters of Jerusalem are first and foremost the female inhabitants of the city whose name they bear, just as the 'daughters of Shiloh' (Judg. 21.21) are the female inhabitants of that place. Robert, Tournay and Feuillet (1963: 70) suggest that the designation originates in the personification of the community as 'mother'. They point out that Jerusalem, or rather Zion, is frequently described as 'mother' to its 'sons' and 'daughters' in the writings of the post-exilic prophets (Isa. 51.20; 60.4; Lam. 1.4).

Although the daughters of Jerusalem are absent from the Old Testament apart from the Song (1.5; 2.7; 3.5, 10; 5.8, 16; 8.4), the daughters of Zion, which is another name for them (3.11), are mentioned in Isa. 3.16-24. There, they are criticized by the prophet on account of their pride:

> The Lord said;
> because the daughters of Zion are haughty
> and walk with outstretched necks,
> glancing wantonly with their eyes,
> mincing along as they go,
> tinkling with their feet;
> the Lord will smite with a scab
> the heads of the daughters of Zion,
> and the Lord will lay bare their secret parts

On the basis of this kind of characterization, Keel (1986: 56) assumes that the daughters of Jerusalem were the young, eligible women of the day, pampered and preoccupied with beauty and love like the women depicted in nineteenth-century French novels. He may well be right, but in fact very little information is given about them by the Song. There, they remain anonymous and undifferentiated. Indeed on the only occasion on which they are invited to participate in the woman's love story (5.8), they appear to be not only sceptical (5.9) but also rather stupid (6.1), offering to respond to her request for help only when her lover has already been found (6.2).

As Robert, Tournay and Feuillet (1963: 70) and Murphy (1990: 84) have suggested, the daughters of Jerusalem are a dramatic trait, a literary device which enables the woman to explore her feelings more fully. If they are silent and unresponsive, revealing none of their feelings or values, it is only so that she can better articulate her own.

The daughters of Jerusalem are addressed for the first time in 1.5-6. The woman uses the pretext of their curiosity to introduce herself (1.5ab). She then proceeds to give a resumé of her family circumstances, for their fascination with her swarthy complexion (1.6ab) is accompanied by the need to explain herself (1.6cd). Of the daughters of Jerusalem we know no more, except that they are not like her. They do however form a close parallel to her brothers, for the woman perceives herself to be equally strange to both parties (1.6). The passage ends, however, not with the daughters of Jerusalem nor with the woman's brothers, but with the heroine of the Song (1.6e) who has never ceased to occupy the centre of the stage.

In her analysis of the structure of the Song, Elliott (1989: 36-41) has underlined the importance of strict refrains in determining the broad lines of formal structure and of variant refrains in linking the sub-divisions within it. Apart from the break after 5.1, dividing the Song into two almost equal parts, and that which follows 6.3, every other major break in the text is constituted by an address to the daughters of Jerusalem, most often in the form of refrain (3.5), and sometimes a double refrain (2.6-7; 8.3-4). The result is not only to signal a transition in the text and to provide a link between parts but also to open up the lovers to the wider world of which they are part, to make the first step in the retelling of the love story.

The final position of these refrains addressed to the daughters of Jerusalem has a bearing on how we read the sequences which precede, for on these occasions the Song seems to be at once experienced with great immediacy by the lovers who address each other directly, and to be related to the daughters of Jerusalem as if these events already belonged to the past. This is the effect of the adjuration refrain referred to above. To these adjurations therefore we now turn.

2.6 may be read as an expression of longing, the continuation of the lovesickness theme of 2.5. This is the reading proposed by the RSV:

> O that his left hand held my head
> and that his right hand embraced me!

Alternatively 2.6 may indicate that the longing which moves the woman to ask for apples and raisin cakes in 2.5 is satisfied by his embrace in the following verse:

His left hand holds my head
and his right hand embraces me.[13]

The first reading invites the reader to conclude that the entire sequence (2.1-7), beginning with a dialogue between the lovers (2.1-3), is voiced in the presence of the daughters of Jerusalem. It is they who are asked to provide apples and raisin cakes in her lover's absence (2.5), they who witness her longing for his embrace (2.6) and they who finally receive the warning not to awaken love too soon (2.7). According to this reading it is their presence, rather than simply the stylistic technique of enallage,[14] which explains her use of the third person in 2.3cdff. If the dialogue of 2.1-2 actually belongs to reported speech, however, it is the purpose of the sequence to make the lovers' words live 'now'.

On the basis of the second reading, the verse is paradoxical for it suggests that the woman is both absorbed in the lovers' self-contained world and in dialogue with the wider world, most likely the daughters of Jerusalem, whom she addresses directly in the very next verse (2.7). It may be that once more we are to understand them to be the silent witnesses to a much longer sequence in which her fervour is capable of making him present to her.

The next appearance of the adjuration—again in full—is in 3.5, following the narration of the woman's search for her lover (3.1-4). It begins in the complete tense (3.4) and moves into the incomplete tense (3.4), as if to suggest that the search which seemed to belong to the past (3.1-3) is only now coming to an end. Here, once more, the daughters of Jerusalem are the means by which past experience becomes present; for the telling of the tale conjures up the presence of her lover so forcibly, that even now she endeavours to bring him home (3.4).

The adjuration appears in abridged form in 5.8. Preceding it is a narrative which describes a second night search (5.1-7), a search characterized by greater violence and less success than the first (3.1-4). She

13. Certain stylistic features favour this translation and with it an unexpected change of scene. These are the self-sufficiency of 2.6 and the way in which the scene appears to come to a close in 2.5c: an inclusio with 2.1 is created by the final word (*'anî*) of 2.5c and a third colon (2.5c) breaks the binary pattern which has dominated thus far (2.1-4). Moreover, the final colon (2.5c) is explanatory: it rounds off the section by stating the cause of the requests previously made (2.5ab).

14. Enallage is the technique whereby a shift takes place between the second and third person forms of address, for example, in Ps. 23.1-3, 4-5, 6. It may also explain the use of the third person in 2.3ab.

ends the tale with a summons to the daughters of Jerusalem which begins in the manner of previous adjurations, 'I adjure you...' (5.8). It fails to reach its term however, for her lover is absent. Hence, it is the motif of sickness (cf. 2.5c) which ensues. As in 2.5, it describes her longing. For the first time, however, the daughters of Jerusalem respond to the adjuration. They do so with slight scepticism, asking her what is so special about her lover that she should be so distraught by his absence (5.9). This question permits her to embark for the first and only time upon a lengthy description of him (5.10-16). She does so in the manner of the descriptive songs (*wasfs*) by means of which he also praises her (4.1-5; 7.1-5). That they fail to co-operate with her is a matter of indifference, for the importance of their presence lies in what their reticence allows her to say.[15] So present does he become to her in the course of the description that, when the daughters of Jerusalem are finally convinced of his worth and offer to help her find him (6.1), she summarily dismisses them, and withdraws with him, at least in her imagination, to their private world (6.2-3). Her sharp words to the daughters of Jerusalem conveniently bring the sequence to a conclusion.

It is noteworthy that in this passage the presence of the daughters of Jerusalem (5.8, 9; 6.1) binds together several different genres—a narrative (5.2-7), a descriptive song (5.10-16) and a poem in praise of their unity (6.2-3). In addition to the cohesion which they create as listeners, therefore, they also strongly assist the structural unity of the Song.

The final occasion on which the woman challenges the daughters of Jerusalem is 8.4. There, as in 2.7, the adjuration follows immediately upon a description of his embrace (cf. 2.6), itself apparently the realization of a longing for his presence, expressed in terms of wanting to take him to her mother's house (8.2). As in 2.7, the adjuration effectively closes the scene.[16]

Each of the above-mentioned adjurations suggests retrospectively that the audience addressed by the woman is the daughters of Jerusalem, even if these passages are primarily soliloquies (3.1-5, 7-11; 5.2-8, 10-16;

---

15. Comparable is the Sumerian song *Message of Ludingira to his Mother* (Cooper 1971: 157-62). In this song a messenger is charged to deliver a greeting to the poet's mother. In order that he will recognize her, the poet engages in a lyrical description of the woman in question. The 'second sign' is particularly close in terms of its imagery to 5.10-16.

16. Exum, on the other hand, understands the adjuration to open units in 2.7 and 8.4 (1973: 53-54, 74).

6.2) or dialogues with her lover (6.1-3). Other passages too bear tell-tale signs of belonging to reported speech. The quoting phrase, 'My beloved spoke, saying to me' (2.10) is just enough to indicate that the verses are conveyed secondhand and that the events described consequently belong to the past. Their power however—like the passages preceding the adjurations—lies in their immediacy, in their capacity to convey the importance of the present moment, the lovers' 'now'. If they are reported to the daughters of Jerusalem, therefore, it is not to relegate them to past experience, but to set them in a context which enables them to live again.

The role of the daughters of Jerusalem in making the lovers' dialogue live again perhaps gives us a clue as to the utilization of the Song in the ancient world, namely as a dramatic poem with several voices. Thus far we have seen how the mere presence of the daughters of Jerusalem constitutes an opportunity for their confidante to tell her love story. We also detect their voice alongside those of the two lovers in the recitation of the same. It is clearly they, for example, who respond to the woman in 5.9 and 6.1 and most likely they who take up the dialogue in 3.6 and 6.10. A number of indices enable us to come to this conclusion. As regards 3.6, the verse follows immediately upon an adjuration addressed to the daughters of Jerusalem. It also takes the form of a question which permits the subsequent elaborate evocation of a royal wedding cortège in response. This kind of intervention is typical of the daughters of Jerusalem if we may be guided by 5.9 and 6.1. As regards 6.10, the rhetorical question, 'Who is this...?' is typical of the kind of praise attributed to the heroine of the Song by the women of the court of which the daughters are part (6.9).[17] It is therefore most likely that it is the daughters of Jerusalem who in 6.10 are the speakers.

If the daughters of Jerusalem are a kind of choir who call the Song forth, acting as a catalyst both to her memories and to her longings, they are also the chief target of its message, for this meditation upon love, its joys and sorrows, is didactic in so far as it issues a severe warning not to awaken love too soon (2.7; 3.5; 8.4). Indeed the poet reinforces his warning with a reflection (8.6-7) upon the power of love to overcome

17. Other voices, unidentified by the poet and incompatible with either of the main characters or with the daughters of Jerusalem, do also appear. Since the daughters of Jerusalem are themselves addressed in 3.11, 3.6-11 is attributed to a narratorial voice. Similarly, the parallel with a dancer at an army camp in 7.1cd suggests that the 'we' of 7.1b refers to a male chorus.

death itself. Like the little sister (8.8-9), the daughters of Jerusalem are perhaps those who will next experience love's transforming power. So wonderful and so terrible an experience is it, warns the woman of the Song, that they should not be tempted to court love aforetime.

Oils, Scents and Spices

The ancient linguistic association of fragrance, breath and life in the Old Testament, is perhaps the reason why fragrance was chosen in ancient Israel as the medium by means of which to designate kings and to praise God. Kings were anointed (*mšḥ*, 1 Sam. 10.1; 2 Sam. 2.4, 5.3; 1 Kgs 1.39) as a sign of the spirit of God that had come upon them (1 Sam. 16.13) and holy oil was spread over the ark and sacred vessels to mark them out as consecrated (Exod. 30.23-25). Because of the association of fragrance with life, oils embalmed the bodies of the dead (Lk. 23.56) and the burning of incense was believed to chase away unwanted demons (Tob. 8.2-3). In the secular world, fragrance was used to honour one's guests, whose head or feet were anointed (Ps. 23.5; Lk. 7.46). It was also used by women to delight their menfolk (Est. 2.12). At Ugarit, Anat's attendants anoint her to prepare her for battle (*KTU* 1.3 ii 1, 3). In each case, sacred or secular, fragrance is a metaphor for life whose dimensions surpass the merely material, visible world. St Paul's reference to the 'fragrance' of Christ pervading the universe (2 Cor. 2.14) is evocative of the particular power of fragrance to convey the innermost essence of a person, to convey that which is intangible and invisible yet particular and unmistakable.

In the evocation of the loved one, therefore, it is not surprising that oils and spices play an important role. Two passages bear comparison because of the similarity of images, namely 1.2b-3a and 4.10b-d. Both passages describe the intimacy of the lovers. In each case, the motif of wine is a symbol of their erotic experience, focused in the exchange of kisses. The reference to the fragrance of each other's oils indicates the proximity of their bodies. The noun *dodîm* alerts us to the fact that it is not love in the abstract with which we are concerned here but rather acts of love, evoked by images of taste and smell (Fox 1985: 97). While the drinking of each other's wine suggests the communion of their bodies, the scent of each other's fragrance expresses the communion of their selves, an exchange which takes place even in the absence of the loved one (1.2). The fragrance of his anointing oils which she enjoys in the intimacy of his company (4.10) is the very same fragrance evoked by the mere mention of his name (1.3).

Of the images described above, 1.3 deserves special attention, for here fragrance is a metaphor for the way in which the lovers are irresistibly drawn to each other by love. In this verse, the very mention of his name is balm to her (1.3b), conveying his presence to her and lifting her spirits. So powerful is this fragrance that not only she but her companions are captivated by it (1.3c). Their response to the scent of his oils is to love him (1.3c). Her response is yet more decisive; she longs to be drawn into his presence (1.4a). The reciprocal movement conveyed by the image of 1.3 is of great eloquence.

When it is the liquid consistency of the oils rather than their scent that is emphasized, the language is powerfully evocative of desire. As the woman reaches for the door in order to open to her lover, her hands 'drip with myrrh' and her fingers run 'with liquid myrrh' (5.5). Similarly, when she describes her lover's lips, she sees them as water-lilies which 'drip liquid myrrh' (5.13). The water-lilies, with which his lips are compared, are associated with erotic experience in 6.2. This is brought about under the cover of a pastoral scene which simply transposes the language of eating and drinking to its pastoral correlate, the language of feeding or grazing.

Normally, one would not let myrrh, imported at great cost from Arabia and India, simply drip (*ntp*), for myrrh was a highly valued commodity, and, among other things,[18] a component of holy oil (Exod. 30.23-25). The image of dripping myrrh is therefore one of gratuitous abundance. It describes a love which can no longer be contained.

The imagery of oils and spices stands on the threshold of two worlds, the courtly milieu and the realm of nature. As the section 1.12-14 discloses, there is a teasing interplay between these two. This fluidity is part of a larger network of teasing transformations which undermine the boundaries between image and referent, inside and outside, the human body and the natural setting. The section begins with a straightforward description of the king who is lying on his couch (1.12). The image is a regal one, the setting, an interior. As he reclines in kingly splendour, a fragrance, that of the nard with which she has anointed herself, pervades

---

18. It was used in rites of purification (Est. 2.12), as an anaesthetic (Mk 15.23) and to embalm the bodies of the dead (Jn 19.39). It was also offered as a gift (Mt. 2.11), used as domestic perfume (Prov. 7.17) and used to scent the robes of the king (Ps. 45.8).

the atmosphere (1.12). A certain distance is maintained between the lovers, for she is present only implicitly, through the scent of her nard, whose costliness befits a king.

In the following verse (1.3), however, she moves progressively to the centre of the stage and it is she who lies down, cradling her lover between her breasts. He is represented metaphorically as a sachet of myrrh, an image called forth by the nard with which she anointed herself. The minimal reference to an external setting has also given way to a metaphorical one. Instead of the couch, her breasts become his resting-place for the night.

A third image offers an alternative to the sachet of myrrh (1.13a). He is to her 'a spray of henna blossoms' (1.14a). The image is apt for not only is henna blossom fragrant but sprigs of henna were commonly worn in the hair and bosoms of young girls in the Middle East, up until the nineteenth century (Möldenke 1952: 125).

With this image a transformation takes place. Oils and spices, the costly products proper to the court, are integrated into their natural setting, for the couch of the king fades before the vineyards of Ein-Gedi (1.14b). The exact intention of the geographical reference is ambiguous. It may simply serve to specify the source of the henna blossom and evoke, by mention of Ein-Gedi, the luxuriance of an oasis which was known for its aromatic plants and trees. It may alternatively aim to indicate a shift in setting, from the court to the country, which has already taken place.

Our unpreparedness for these transformations and our inability to clearly discern metaphor from referent again and again takes us by surprise. The breaking of linguistic boundaries and the all but complete disintegration of distinctions mirror, at a linguistic level, the fusion of the lovers who nevertheless remain themselves. Such a journey is characterized by delight and surprise, the very same sensations which the reader experiences in reading the Song.

At the midpoint of the Song is 'a garden locked, a fountain sealed' (4.12b). It is the woman who is here represented as a garden. She is this intimate, enclosed, private space, accessible to her lover alone. She it is who gathers within her all that is representative of the luxuriance and fertility of the natural world. All the splendour and beauty of the natural world is for a moment concentrated in her. Each spice mentioned in the Song, henna, nard, myrrh and frankincense, is present in this garden. Indeed within its walls grow many more exotic aromatic plants and trees—cinnamon, sweet cane, saffron[19] and aloes. Piled up one upon the other without further explanation, they create the impression of heady luxuriance.

The motif of the garden tells with infinite discretion the story of love's consummation, yet it is also strangely continuous with the perpetual springtime of the garden of the world which everywhere declares the wonder of this singular love (2.11-13; 6.11; 7.11-12). At the end of the poem this continuity is made explicit in so far as the garden which represents the woman suddenly becomes the real garden to which she invites her lover to come (5.1). There, he may gather what is reserved specifically for him, his 'myrrh' and his 'spices' (5.1).

The effect of this two-tiered metaphorical system is to affirm that not only is the beauty of creation present in her in a unique way, at least in the eyes of her lover, but that her presence pervades the world. Thus it is that even when he absents himself from her to flee to the 'mountain of myrrh, and to the hill of frankincense' (4.6) or to the unnamed 'mountains of spices' (8.14) we know that she is also there. The density of scents and spices in the aromatic garden alludes to an intimacy which cannot be enjoyed when absent from one another. Their separation however cannot prevent the perpetuity of a certain communion. It lingers as a perfume which is diffused everywhere. It is on this note that the Song ends (8.14).

A final note on the beds of spices of 5.13 and 6.2. In 5.13[20] the reference is a straightforward metaphor used to describe his cheeks. It becomes intelligible in the second colon when these beds of spices are said to be fragrant. The language of fragrance is again evocative of the intimacy of the lovers.

In 6.2 on the other hand, these beds of spices become part of the universe the lovers inhabit. Already the mention of the garden (6.2a) is enough to alert us to a possible erotic overtone contained in the reference, for the motif of the garden is powerfully used in this manner. Our intuitions are confirmed by the juxtaposition of a declaration of

---

19. *karkom* is a *hapax legomenon*, generally thought to refer to saffron.

20. (k^e)*migd^{e}lôt*, 'towers', has been revocalized to correspond to the feminine plural *piel* participle *m^{e}gadlôt*, from the root *gdl*, 'to grow' (*piel*). 'Towers of fragrance' makes little sense in the context in spite of the suggestion of Loretz (1964: 36) and Gerleman (1964: 175) that the reference is to perfume bottles. Moreover, the revocalized reading enhances the parallelism with 5.13d: both 5.13b and 5.13d are characterized by participial phrases.

their love for one another (6.3a) with a pastoral image (6.3b) which is reminiscent of those other references to eating and drinking. They are evidently erotic (1.2; 2.3; 4.5, 10; 5.1; 7.9; 8.2). Are the beds of spices actual beds of spices or are they metaphors for something rather different? Again it is the lovers' prerogative to play tricks on us.

Veils and Mantles

Any reference to clothing is related to the woman only. She is adorned with jewels by her lover as a sign of his affection for her (1.10-11).

Articles of clothing, and in particular veils, also serve to elaborate another theme however, namely that of her inwardness, her hiddenness, her reluctance to be drawn out of doors. Landy (1983: 68, 72) draws attention to this essential difference between the lovers. She is characterised by interiority and by stability, while he is restless, caught in a perpetual movement which precipitates him from the 'mountains of spice' (8.14) to her side. Again and again he comes to his coy beloved, coaxing her to leave with him. He comes to her window (2.9), addresses her as a dove hidden in the clefts of the rock (2.14) and knocks on the door, even tries the latch (5.4). She, on the other hand, conceives of their love differently. Rather than escape out of doors, she more often dreams of drawing him to a yet more intimate enclosed space, the house of her mother, indeed the chamber of her own conception (3.4, 8.2).

It is to this difference between the lovers that her veil relates. She remains for him mysteriously hidden, wondrously inaccessible, inviting him to discover someone who is at once familiar and strangely unknown. It is no coincidence that the first reference to her veil is associated with her eyes. It is their perfect clarity which her veil, for a moment, masks (4.1). The image, as it is presented in 4.1, is extremely terse yet it is laden with allusion. It refers not only to the coy reserve of the doves of 2.14ab but also to his desire to hear her voice and to see her face (2.14cd).

The same word, *ṣammâ*, is used on two other occasions (4.3, 6.7).[21] On each occasion the veil masks the woman's cheeks[22] which are rosy

21. Apart from the Song, the word appears in Isa. 47.2 only. It has been related to the Aramaic root *ṣamṣem*, to veil (Pope 1977: 457).

22. *raqqâ* refers to the 'temple' in Judg. 4.21-22; 5.36. Here, however, the term most likely refers to a more extensive area encompassing her cheeks which are as

as a pomegranate. The meshwork of the veil is described in terms of the composition of this fruit whose seeds are encased in tiny cells of rosy flesh. The image falls in sequences which strongly parallel each other (4.1-3; 6.5-7). Indeed they are identical, except for a greater precision regarding the sheep which are shorn in 4.2, and in the addition of a description of her lips in 4.3a. The first sequence is part of a *wasf* which proceeds from her eyes (4.1b) to her breasts (4.5). The second sequence is briefer, dependent on the imagery of the first. The additions to the first sequence are carefully chosen, for the images used to describe her lips (4.3a) and her cheeks (4.3b) are both drawn from the realm of haberdashery. In this way one image makes way for another; the scarlet thread which marks the meeting of her lips (4.3a) prepares for the veil which covers her cheeks (4.3b). The images are also related by colour; the scarlet thread finds a ready correspondent in her rosy cheeks.

The image of the veil may belong specifically to wedding imagery, as does the term of address, *kallâ*, 'bride' (4.9, 11, 12; 5.1), for although the Song is not concerned with marriage as such, it is possible that elements are drawn from the marriage ceremony in order to celebrate love. The evidence of the Hebrew Bible is that although veils were not normally worn by women in public, young women did temporarily veil themselves when betrothed (De Vaux 1935: 408). Rebecca, for example, who did not previously wear a veil (Gen. 24.16) covers herself as soon as she sees Isaac to whom she is promised (Gen. 24.65). This custom explains why it was possible for Laban to substitute Leah for Rachel at Jacob's expense (Gen. 29.23-25).

Alternately, the image may derive from life in a particularly sophisticated milieu. Isaiah (Isa. 3.18-23) bears witness to the fact that, in this environment, many kinds of headdress were worn. These include the $r^e d\hat{\imath}d$ of 5.7, a light summer mantle.[23] Eighth-century Assyrian sculptures from Sennacherib's palace in Nineveh also testify to the fact (Keel 1986: 178). There, the women of Judah are depicted wearing a kind of veil which covers their hair and falls down over the shoulders to the ground.

Veils, however, were never prescribed as female dress in Judaism. Normally Hebrew women appeared in public unveiled. Only thus could Abraham's servant see that Rebecca was 'very fair to look upon' (Gen.

rosy as a pomegranate (see Robert, Tournay and Feuillet 1963: 163; Fox 1985: 130; Murphy 1990: 155).

23. The word used by LXX is θεριστρον.

24.16), only thus was Rebecca's beauty a matter of concern for Isaac when they lived among the people of Gerar (Gen. 26.7), only thus was Abraham concerned for Sarah when they travelled among the Egyptians (Gen. 12.10-16). Moreover there is no specific word in the Talmud for a veil and the Mishnah (*m. Šab.* 6.6) cedes to the practice by way of a concession to those women living in an Arab environment, where veils were normally worn (De Vaux 1935: 397-412). It is to this practice to which Tertullian refers, when he recommends that Christian virgins should veil themselves for the sake of modesty (*De Virginibus Velandis*).

It appears then that, contrary to the practice of their neighbours, Hebrew women wore veils only in specific circumstances, on the occasion of a young woman's marriage and for ornamental purposes, in sophisticated and cosmopolitan milieux.

There is, however, one other circumstance, that of prostitution, in which the veil was worn. Genesis 38 tells the story of Tamar who, in order to appear to be a harlot, not only sat by the roadside but also covered herself in a veil. Indeed it is the donning of the veil which, in Judah's mind, identifies her as a harlot (Gen. 38.15). The word used to describe Tamar's veil is *ṣaʿîp*, from the verb *ṣʿp*, 'to fold', 'to double'. This would suggest that the veil consisted of two parts, leaving room for the eyes. It is this word too which describes Rachel's veil (Gen. 24.65).

This is not the vocabulary of the Song. In 1.7-8, however, the urgency of the woman's search for her lover is perhaps enough to suggest that the participle *ʿoṭᵉyâ*, literally 'as one wrapped', might allude to harlotry (Delitzsch 1875: 10). Must she also go to such lengths to receive his attention? Must she, like Tamar, also deceive him to remind him of his duty towards her?

A number of other solutions have been proposed, each of which dulls this extremely powerful metaphor. Driver (1974: 159-60), for example, proposes that there is a second root *ʿṭh*, used in Jer. 43.12, of a shepherd delousing a garment. Interpreted accordingly, the image would convey her boredom in his absence and her total lack of interest in those around her. The infrequence of the meaning of this root however works against this interpretation.

An alternative is to follow the Peshitta, Vg and Symmachus. Each of these recognizes in the form *keʿoṭᵉyâ* the metathesis of the first two consonants. The verb, they argue, is not *ʿṭh*, to 'wrap up', but *ṭʿh*, 'to wander'. To translate 'as one who wanders' fits well with the context except that it conveys nothing of her desperation. Only a straight-forward translation of the MT can do this. It does so by means of allusion to a practice known to us only by virtue of the Tamar story of Genesis 38.

Haulotte (1966: 11-13) has drawn our attention to the deeper significance of dress in the Hebrew Bible and to the symbolic dimensions of certain actions, such as the putting on or taking off clothes. On two occasions in the Song (5.3, 7), clothing is a medium of symbolic action. Both of these occurrences fall in the second narrative sequence (5.2-8).

The sequence opens with a paradoxical statement which discloses her constant attentiveness to her lover: 'I slept, but my heart was awake' (5.2a). Hence it is both surprise and relief which her exclamation evokes, 'Listen! My beloved is knocking!' (5.2b). He then calls to her directly, asking her to let him in (5.2c-f). A moment's hesitation on her part (5.3) is enough to provoke the failure of their meeting, for the time it takes her to consider her present state of undress and what she would have to do to receive him is the time it takes him to put his hand into the key-hole and to withdraw it again (5.4a).

The consequences of her hesitation are deeply ironic, for she, who is thrown into disarray at the thought of being already undressed when her lover comes to her door (5.3), is thereafter forced to leave her home in the middle of the night to be forcibly stripped of her mantle (5.7). The inconvenience of having to get dressed again to open the door and to find shoes for her freshly bathed feet (5.3) is nothing compared to the violence she subsequently suffers at the hands of the nightwatchmen (5.7). The removal of clothing is at the heart of the tragedy, both its cause and the nature of its effect.

In each case the removal of clothing itself is very different. In 5.3 it is she herself who undresses. She takes off her tunic (*kuttonet*), that is, a kind of petticoat (Haulotte 1966: 27-28). She is thereby rendered very vulnerable, as vulnerable as Tamar who was banished from the house of Amnon and sent outside wearing only her petticoat (2 Sam. 13.18). Vulnerability however may also accompany anticipation, for the bathing of her feet lends suggestive overtones to the theme of uncovering. It does so due to the well known euphemistic connotations of uncovering one's feet in the ancient world (Judg. 3.24; 2 Kgs 18.27 *qere*; Isa. 6.2).

In 5.7 on the other hand, the removal of clothing is a consequence of violence and deliberate injury.[24] In this matter she has no choice, for she is simply the passive victim of assault. Here, the clothing removed is outer clothing. According to the LXX, it is a light summer mantle.

Gemstones and Precious Metals

The first mention of jewellery directs the reader to Egypt, for in 1.9-11 the woman is compared to a mare belonging to the stud of Pharaoh. The image recalls those texts which speak of horses and chariots brought from Egypt during the ostentatious reign of Solomon (1 Kgs 10.26, 29; 2 Chron. 1.17):

> To a mare of Pharaoh's chariotry,
> I compare you, my love.

This simile, introduced so boldly in 1.9, is elaborated by a synonymic pair in 1.10. It is followed by a climactic statement in 1.11 which rounds off the scene. The difficulty however is that the intention of the poet seems to change in the course of these verses, as he increasingly describes the woman directly without the mediation of the simile of the mare. Without any reference to the simile of 1.9, in 1.10 he simply describes the earrings and collar which adorn her:

> Your cheeks, lovely between earrings,
> Your neck through beaded collar.

The influence of the initial comparison survives only metaphorically, in the allusion to the horse's harness which these jewels suggest. Alter (1985: 197) first pointed out this optical illusion; mare and woman shadow each other, tenor and vehicle have become one.

The exact nature of the image is also difficult to determine because of the obscurity of the word *tôrîm*, which most commentators connect with the verb *tôr*, 'to go round' (Pope 1977: 343). On the basis of this etymology, the noun has sometimes been understood to refer to plaits of hair.

Alternatively the noun may refer to earrings, to the bands of a headdress or to locks of a wig (Keel 1986: 64). The large gold loop earrings worn by the women of the eighteenth dynasty, as described by

---

24. Her violation is reminiscent of those prophetic passages in which Yahweh 'strips' those whom he punishes of their apparel (Isa. 20.4; 47.1-3; Jer. 13.22).

Wilkinson (1971: 121-22), would fit well in this context. Circularity is implied by the etymology of the term.

Egyptian jewellery may also shed light on another term, *harûzîm* (1.10b), a technical term not found elsewhere in the Old Testament, but which is used of stringing pearls or fish in postbiblical Hebrew. Pope (1977: 344) argues that in Arabic the verb is used of stitching, while the noun denotes a piece of jewellery composed of beads which is worn around the neck. In Egypt, beaded collars were frequently worn both by men and women. Two types of such collars are described by Wilkinson (1971: 108), the *usekh* and the *shebin*. Keel (1986: 64), on the other hand, draws attention to the necklaces composed of several rows of pearls which were frequently found in Syria. He cites the example of an ivory found in Nimrud in north Syria, dating from the ninth or eighth century BCE. It depicts a woman wearing a necklace composed of a number of strings of beads worn tightly around the neck.

The translation proposed in this study abandons the postbiblical Hebrew association with pearls in order to evoke a more traditional style of necklace, the collar. This is because it is not so much the materials used that the image highlights as the composition of the necklace. The Hebrew is extremely terse. The *hapax harûzîm* simply indicates something that is formed by perforation and strung together, that is, beads. The term 'collar' gives the image an Egyptian flavour, appropriate to the reference to Pharaoh in 1.9.

1.11 compounds and develops the imagery of the preceding verse, indicating by means of the merismatic pair 'gold and silver' the costliness of the earrings and consequently the esteem in which the wearer is held.[25] The imagery is reminiscent of Psalm 45 in which the queen on her wedding day 'stands in gold of Ophir' (Ps. 45.9). The introduction of the first person plural form 'we' indicates something of the woman's influence. It is a climactic device, parallel to that used by the heroine when, in 1.4, she invokes the support of her companions in praise of her loved one.

Noteworthy also is the choice of adjective used to describe her beauty in 1.10a. Her cheeks are described as *na'wû*, an adjective which echoes her self-proclaimed splendour in 1.5a. The use of the adjective *na'wê* in

---

25. *n^equddôt* is also a *hapax legomenon* although other forms derived from the same root may be translated 'speckled' or 'spotted' in Gen. 30.32, 35.39 and by 'crumbs' in Josh. 9.5 and 1 Kgs 14.3. In the context of Song 1.11, however, 'spangles' is more appropriate.

1.5 and 1.10 discloses the unpromising outsider to be in fact a treasured beauty.

Ornamental imagery comes to the fore in 3.9-10c. One of the key words, *'appiryôn* (3.9), is a *hapax* though the general consensus is that it is a loanword related to the Greek word *phoreion* (LXX), 'a sedan chair'. Moreover it parallels the West Semitic word *miṭṭâ*, 'a couch' or 'bed' which, as in 1 Sam. 19.15, seems to be portable.

In 3.9, the focus changes from the escort, which accompanies Solomon's litter (3.7bc-8), to a description of the royal palanquin itself. Since the exact nature of the *'appiryôn* is unknown, so too is the exact nature of its component parts and its ornamentation. It is however obvious that the description is hyperbolic. Only the best materials are used in a litter which honours the king. Comparable is the description of the gifts given to Asherah (*KTU* 1.4, 129-40).

The first material to be mentioned is wood from Lebanon (3.9). The reference is probably to the cedar wood for which Lebanon was so well known. These are the trees which on account of their strength (Ps. 29.5), height (2 Kgs 19.23) and majesty (1 Kgs 4.33; 2 Kgs 14.9; Zech. 11.1) display the magnificence of Yahweh's kingship. It is entirely fitting that they should be used to build the framework of the litter belonging to the king.

Next comes a description of its 'pillars' (3.10) which, depending on the nature of the vehicle described, could either be the supports of the canopy or the legs on which the entire frame rests, if it has legs. These are either solid silver or have silver inlay.

Parallel to the description of these pillars is the description of its *rᵉpîdâ*, (3.10b), variably translated by *anakliton* (LXX), *reclinatorium* (Vg) by the ancients and by 'bolster' (Pope), 'carpets' (Fox), 'floor' (Falk) and 'roof' (Murphy) in our own day. This noun, also a *hapax*, comes from the verb *rpd*, 'to spread' or 'to stretch out', and has been translated by 'roof' in this version. The reason is stylistic; together the pillars and the roof constitute the framework. That is surely why they appear as a pair in 3.10ab. Only in 3.10c does the description pass to the inside of the litter, first to the seat (3.10c) and then to the decoration of the interior as a whole (3.10d).

As the posts are of silver, so the roof is of gold. If the reference is to gold inlay, nevertheless the impression is that of solid gold. As in our own language 'silver and gold' are a common pair (Deut. 7.25; 8.13; 17.17; 1 Kgs 15.15; 2 Kgs 7.8; Isa. 2.7; Ezek. 38.13; Ps. 105.37; 115.4;

135.15), for they constitute the entire range of precious metals accessible to the ancient world. Most often, they characterize regal or cultic splendour. It is the former to which the pair refers in the Song.

The parallelism continues in 3.10cd with reference first to the seat, and then the interior. The seat is made of purple (3.10c), a reference to the cloth rather than simply to the colour. In the ancient world, this expensive fabric was associated with dignity and honour. It furbished the tabernacle (Exod. 25.4) and was worn by royalty and those of high rank (Mk 15.17; Lk. 16.19; Jn 19.2). It is therefore fitting that it should bedeck the litter of the king. The climax of the description however is in the interior, which is inlaid not with silver, gold nor precious fabric, but 'with love' which is the most splendid and honourable of all (cf. 8.7). Emendations have been proposed so as to harmonize 3.10d with the preceding description. *'ahabâ*, 'love', has been emended to *hābnîm*, 'ebony', by Graetz (1871) and to *'ᵃbānîm*, 'stones', by Gerleman (1965). Driver (1936) has even suggested that the noun refers to 'leather' on the basis of Arabic cognate *ihāb*. These emendations however disguise a very significant change in register brought about by the adverbial accusative *'ahabâ*, 'with love', for not only does the splendour of the litter honour Solomon, the owner, but the love with which it was made also honours his bride. Indeed, it is only for love's sake that the description of the royal cortège is present at all, for its primary function is that of an extended metaphor, paying tribute to the lovers, firstly the male lover, whose litter it is, and secondly the woman, who may be hidden inside.

Following a punctual reference to ornamental imagery in 4.9, imagery from this imaginative field is developed in the course of two *waṣfs* or descriptive songs, 5.10-16 and 7.2-7.

Although, in the descriptive songs, it is most often the male lover who describes the woman (4.1-5; 6.4-7; 7.2-7), in 5.10-16 the trend is reversed. Also, whereas the movement in the *wasf* of 7.1-5 is upwards, beginning with her lower regions and culminating in her head and hair, 5.10-16 begins with a general statement concerning her lover's complexion (5.10) and proceeds from a detailed description of his face (5.12-13) and head (5.11) to an evocation of his torso (5.14-15). It is significant that apart from details concerning his face (5.11-12), at which point natural imagery dominates, he is described almost entirely in terms of the costly materials of artistic enterprise—alabaster, gold, ivory and precious stones. There has been much debate as to how to interpret this imagery, depending on whether, with Wittekindt (1926), the imagery refers to a statuette used in the sacred marriage rite, or whether with Gerleman (1965), a statue is used as a metaphor of the woman's beauty.

In response to the cultic reading, it must be acknowledged that the *wasf* or descriptive song, which became so popular in later Arabic love poetry, most likely originated in hymns to the gods and in descriptions of their statuary.[26] The Sumerian hymn, in which Inanna bedecks various parts of her body with jewels and precious stones, probably describes one such statue:

> She picks the buttock-stones, puts them on her buttocks,
> Inanna picks the head-stones, puts them on her head,
> She picks the *duru*-lapis lazuli stones, puts them on her nape,
> She picks ribbons of gold, puts them in her hair of the head,
> She picks the narrow gold earrings, puts them on her ears,
> She picks bronze eardrops, puts them on her ear-lobes...(*ANET*: 638,
> ll. 11-16)

It is clear from the love poetry of Ramesside Egypt, however, that this imagery became the currency of poets, by means of which to speak of the overwhelming splendour of the loved one, for, like the Song of Songs, these songs and poems are concerned with human love rather than the sexuality of the gods. Thus it is that the language of the statuary inherited from ancient hymns to the gods is radically transformed to become part of an enthusiastic description of the loved one.[27]

> Long of neck, white of breast,
> her hair, true lapis lazuli.
> Her arms surpass gold,
> her fingers like lotuses...(Fox 1985: 52)

It is to this end that this hyperbolic language is also used in the Song. If there are hints of artistic models, the poet has cut himself free from their cultic context.

If Gerleman (1965: 68-69) was correct in drawing attention to the metaphorical use of artistic models, the *wasf* cannot, however, be interpreted solely in the light of Egyptian polychrome statuary, for the imagery of 5.10-16 is much more wide ranging than he suggests. While

---

26. Hallo (1970) in particular has drawn attention to the cultic origin of Sumerian poetry.

27. In his discussion of the Old Babylonian text the 'Message of Ludingira' Cooper (1971: 101) points out that there too the description of statuary has become a literary device enabling the poet to sing the mother's praise.

statuary is undoubtedly the inspiration of certain images, these combine with a variety of architectural images to convey both the beauty and the grandeur of her lover. At times, he has the formality of an exceptionally valuable bust (5.10-11). At others, he exhibits the grandeur and solidity of a civic monument (5.15).

The *wasf* begins in 5.10 with a description of his complexion. The adjectives *ṣaḥ* and *'adôm* (5.10) form a hendiadys, translated here by 'bright red'. Gerleman (1965: 69) suggests that the combination *ṣaḥ wᵉ'adôm* makes one think of those bronze figures of Egyptian poly-chromy whose genitals were sometimes inlaid with gold, silver, copper or electron. Keel (1986: 186) on the other hand remarks that in Egyptian art, men were usually painted a red-brown colour, consonant with the Hebrew designation of man as *'adam*, 'the red one' and with the prac-tice, in the Old Testament, of associating masculine beauty with a ruddy complexion (1 Sam. 16.12; 17.42). To his ruddy cheeks, the adjective *ṣaḥ*[28] adds the notion of radiance, remarked by Gerleman in his allusion to Egyptian statuary.

The statuesque quality of the lover is enhanced by the hendiadys of the following verse wherein his head is described as *ketem paz*, 'gold, finest gold', a description reminiscent of the image which Nebuchadnezzar saw in his dream (Dan. 2.32). The aim of the colourful, sculptural imagery of 5.10-11a is to emphasize the virility and surpassing value of the lover. This is made explicit in 5.10b, where he is described as 'outstanding among ten thousand'.

If 5.11a describes the young man's head in general, 5.11b enters into greater detail with the description of his hair. The noun *taltallîm* is a *hapax* which Pope (1977: 536) relates to Akkadian *taltallû*, the pollen of the date panicle.[29] Most scholars have translated the word by 'palm

---

28. In Lam. 4.7, the verbal form refers to the colour, white. Here, the adjective is used as an evocation of that other component of colour which is brightness. As Fox (1985: 147) points out, ideas of whiteness and brightness are both implied in the Egyptian adjective *ḥd*. Indeed both aspects appear in an Egyptian love song cited by Fox (1985: 52) precisely with regard to complexion:

> Behold her like Sothis rising
> at the beginning of a good year:
> shining, precious, white of skin,
> lovely of eyes when gazing.

29. He also points out that, in Arabic, *taltalat* is used of the envelope of the date

fronds' on the basis of this etymology. In the context of the sculptural imagery of 5.10-11a, the image suggests the stylized representation of hair on a piece of statuary. The blackness of his locks (5.11b) adds colour to the portrait, reminding the reader of those Egyptian sculptures described by Gerleman (1965: 26) which, although made of wood or soft stone, were either completely or partly painted.

The introduction of natural imagery in 5.11b does however humanize the static portrait and prepare for the extended metaphor of 5.12. More precisely, the image of the raven (5.11b) calls up the image of the dove, a motif already well known to readers as used of her eyes (1.15; 4.1). With this eye contact, the formality of the portrait is broken and movement is restored to the scene. Two other natural images follow in 5.13, both of which betray her longing to be reunited with her lover. The formal portrait reestablishes itself however as soon as she passes from the description of his eyes and lips to his arms (5.14ab), torso (5.14cd) and legs (5.15). Henceforth her self-control reasserts itself in the measured advance of the *wasf*.

Many suggestions have been made to identify the $g^e lîlê\ z\bar{a}h\bar{a}b$ of 5.14. Derived from the verb *gll*, 'to roll', the form appears twice in 1 Kgs 6.34 of some part of the doors of the inner sanctuary. Pope (1977: 542) suggests that the reference is to folding doors, Fox (1985: 148) suggests that they refer to the hinge bars. The only other occasion on which the form appears is in Est. 1.6 in connection with the hanging of curtains in the royal palace. There, it is translated either by 'rods' or 'rings'. Use of the form elsewhere in the Old Testament therefore suggests an architectural image; her lover's arms[30] display the solidity and durability of rods of pure gold.

The imagery of 5.14a is developed in 5.14b where it is affirmed that these rods of gold are set with precious stones, the identity of which is unknown. Most likely they came from Tarshish, the port which has given them its name. It is known, however, that these gemstones were highly esteemed in so far as they also decorate the high priest's breastplate (Exod. 39.13). Next in sequence is a description of his lumbar area

---

palm and that the comparison of hair to date clusters or to vines also appears in Arabic love poetry (1977: 536).

30. The interpretation of 5.14 is complicated further by by the translation *yadâw*, literally, 'his hands', but more probably referring here to his arms (Gen. 24.30, 37; Jer. 38.12).

(cf. Dan. 2.32)[31] which is likened to a block of ivory,[32] encrusted with lapis lazuli. Murphy (1990: 72 n. 305) compares the imagery to that of a Sumerian love poem concerned with male virility:

> O my pure pillar, my pillar
> Sweet are your charms
> Pillar of alabaster set in lapis lazuli
> Sweet are your charms

Keel (1986: 190), on the other hand, makes the comparison with a twelfth-century hymn to the Egyptian sun god Re:

> His bones are of silver,
> his flesh is of gold,
> what his head is,
> is of real lapis lazuli.

Gerleman (1965: 69) interprets 5.15 in terms of statuary, insisting that the sockets, *'adnîm*, are those of a statue, on which the legs rest like pillars. The primary reference of the imagery, however, is not to statuary, as Gerleman suggests, but to architecture. Indeed the vocabulary of 5.15 recalls the most significant of Israel's buildings; his legs, which are compared to alabaster columns (*'ammudîm*), recall the columns of the tabernacle (Exod. 27.10, 11, 17; 36.38; Num. 3.37), the pillars of Solomon's palace (1 Kgs 7.2, 3, 6) and the pillars before the temple (1 Kgs 7.15; Jer. 52.20, 21; 1 Chron. 18.8; 2 Chron. 3.15, 17; Ezek. 40.49). Moreover, the verb *'sd* is commonly used in the Old Testament for laying the foundation of walls (Ps. 137.7), and in particular those of the temple (Ezra 3.12; Isa. 44.28; 1 Kgs 5.31; Ezra 3.10). It is also used metaphorically of the foundations of the world (Ps. 24.2; 104.5; Prov. 3.19). The sockets into which these pillars are set are also described using an architectural term: *'eden* describes the base of the tabernacle (Exod. 26.19), the base of pillars (Exod. 27.11; Num. 3.36) and metaphorically the base of the earth (Job 38.6). Nor is 5.14 unique in its

---

31. *me'im* usually refers to the internal organs of digestion and procreation, but here the word must surely refer to his stomach or more precisely his loins, since every other element in the description is to an external feature.

32. The noun *'ešet* is a *hapax*, perhaps related to *'šš*, 'to be smooth' (cf. Jer. 5.28) or possibly *'št*, the Aramaic equivalent of *ḥšb*, 'to think of', used of fashioning works of art (Exod. 28.27, 28; 29.5). In rabbinical Hebrew, however, it is used of a 'bar', a 'pillar', or 'block' (*b. Men.* 28a; *Cant. R.* 5.12; see Fox 1985: 149), the reading most appropriate here.

use of architectural imagery to describe a loved one: in Sir. 26.18 the virtuous woman is compared to the golden columns of the tabernacle (Exod. 25.31-40; 26.32).

Nor is the reference in 5.15 to alabaster pillars without precedent, for it recalls the description of the temple in 1 Kings 6–7 (Robert, Tournay and Fouillet 1963: 233) and that of the queen's palace in Est. 1.6 (Pope 1977: 546). In the Akkadian text in which Ludingira describes his mother (Cooper 1971: 160), an alabaster statuette becomes a metaphor for the mother's splendour. She is 'an alabaster statuette, set on a lapis pedestal'.

With the imagery of 5.15cd, the language of art and artisanship, which has dominated the *wasf* (with the exception of 5.12-13), gives way to imagery drawn from the natural world. Indeed the cedars of Lebanon, which describe his appearance, stand on the threshold of these two worlds: they clearly belong to the natural world, yet their wood is the raw material which elsewhere furbishes images of artistry in the Song (1.17; 2.9; 8.9). At this point too the *wasf* itself draws to a close, for complete now is the itemized description of his body from top to toe. Henceforth her considerations are more general. They are evocative of his desirability as a whole; in 5.15cd she describes his overall appearance, in 5.16 she speaks of the sweetness of his speech.

In the *wasf* of 7.2-5 the imagery of art and artisanship constitutes one element among imagery drawn from a multiplicity of sources, natural (7.3d-4), architectural (7.5a) and topographical (7.5-6). Indeed in contrast to the *wasf* of 5.10-16, where this language predominates, here the imagery is limited to the evocation of the woman's thighs and navel,[33] described as the work of artisanship and as a rounded bowl respectively (7.2b-3a). In this *wasf* it is notable how vehicle and tenor collude so as to emphasise the fullness of the woman's form, her voluptuousness, her fecundity. Thus it is that the male lover chooses to focus upon her breasts (7.4) and rounded thighs (7.2), her navel (7.3) and her belly (7.3),

33. On the basis of the Arabic cognate *širr*, meaning 'secret', some have translated 'vulva' or 'pudenda' (Pope 1977: 617-18). Since the same noun appears in Ezek. 16.4 with reference to the umbilical cord, I prefer to translate it by 'navel'. Reference to the iconography of ancient Syria is of further help in understanding the imagery (cf. Keel 1986: 215, fig. 116). There, women are depicted with enlarged navels, suggesting that the navel was considered an attribute of female beauty. Alternatively, Krinetzki (1981: 93) suggests that the navel represents a larger area corresponding to the lower abdomen.

each of which is itself either characterized by, or described in terms of, imagery of circularity: a finely turned bowl (7.3a),[34] a heap of wheat (7.3c), a circle of lilies (7.3d), pools in Heshbon (7.5). In this sequence, only her breasts are described in imagery which is not characterized by the notion of circularity. Here, a familiar image is preferred, that of the fawns, twins of a gazelle (cf. 4.5).

The Song reaches its climax in 8.6-8, at which point the woman, for the first time, reflects upon the experience of love. She introduces a general statement about the inexorable power of love (8.6c-d) with an urgent imperative and a simile belonging to the imaginative field of ornamental imagery (8.6a-b):

> Set me as a seal upon your heart,
> as a seal upon your arm

By means of the first of these images, the woman expresses her desire never to be separated from her lover, to be present with him in all his actions, for the metaphor refers to those seals of metal or of stone which were either worn on a cord around the neck (Gen. 38.18) or worn as a ring on the hand (Gen. 41.42; Jer. 22.24).[35] A similar image appears in an Egyptian love song:[36]

> If only I were her little seal ring,
> the keeper of her finger,
> I would see her love
> each and every day (Fox 1985: 38)

Whereas in the first image, the metaphor concerns a seal worn around her lover's neck, in the second image the metaphor concerns the capacity of the seal to authenticate the ownership of the object which bears its mark. The woman not only wants to be ever present with him, but she desires to be imprinted upon his arm, that is to be ever more

---

34. *'aggan* is used only twice elsewhere, in Exod. 24.6 and Isa. 22.24. In both contexts it refers to a container. *agannu*, in Akkadian, designates a bowl. As regards the adjective *hassahar*, which is also a *hapax*, LXX and Vg both translate by 'turned'.

35. The image appears elsewhere in the Hebrew Bible as a symbol of the loyalty which binds Yahweh to his servant Zerubbabel in Hag. 2.23 and Sir. 4.9. It is an image of the destruction of this complicity as regards Coniah, son of Jehoiakim (Jer. 22.24) who proves to be an unwilling servant. In Gen. 38.18, 25, in the story of Tamar and Judah, the seal or signet ring is the token of the integrity of its owner.

36. The Egyptian origin of the image is further substantiated by Pope (1966: 666) who argues that the word *hôtam*, used in 8.6, is an Egyptian loanword.

closely united with him, bone of his bone, flesh of his flesh (cf. Gen. 2.23). The image derives from the marking of an amphora with the seal of its owner, comparable to the marking of livestock in our own day.

The close of this section bears the sting in the tail (8.7):

> ...if someone were to offer for love,
> all the wealth of his house,
> he would be laughed to scorn.

The paradox is that however appropriate the images of wealth, splendour and influence may be in the evocation of the lovers' relationship, as has been demonstrated throughout this section, they are nevertheless insufficient to express the worth of love. All wealth and power pales into insignificance before the absolute power of love which is itself its own reward. Only lovers, says the Song, comprehend love's worth. Only fools, the Song insists, persist in bargaining for love. This silver cannot buy (8.12). The image of silver, essential to discourse concerning Solomon and his vineyards in the closing verses (8.11-12), presses home this triumphant conclusion.

Architectural Details

This section belongs to the larger subject of topography which will be considered in due course. The present task is merely to draw attention to those images which speak of the lovers, and particularly of the woman, in architectural terms.

First of all there is the reversal of the woman's social position. Initially she is set in opposition to the daughters of Jerusalem (1.5), city dwellers who despise her country ways. Later she is beaten by the defenders of its gates, the watchmen of its walls (5.7). In 8.10, however, she sings her song of triumph using imagery based upon urban architecture. She, who was seen as a danger to those living within the city walls (5.7), is herself a wall (8.10). She, who no doubt was spied upon from its towers, boasts of breasts which resemble them (8.10). The city no longer threatens her. Instead its walls and towers rise triumphant in love's praise.

More precise are the architectural details of the *wasf* of 7.2-7. They appear with particular concentration in 7.5. There, her neck is compared to an ivory tower (7.5a). Her eyes are compared to pools in Heshbon by a certain gate of Bath-rabbim (7.5bc). Her nose is compared to a tower in Lebanon, overlooking Damascus (7.5de). As the *wasf* proceeds, the poet's vision becomes progressively broader as architectural details consistently cede to topographical ones: pools (7.5b) and gates (7.5c) yield to allusions to the city of Damascus (7.5e) and to Mount Carmel (7.6a). A second consequence of this progression is to identify the woman both with particular locations in Palestinian towns and with the wider world of the ancient Near East. Local, national and international boundaries become indistinct. She, who is powerfully present in particular places, by a certain pool or gate, also seems to pervade much of the known world.

The progression of 7.2-7 is a logical one. The *wasf* moves upward from feet (7.2a) to thighs (7.2c), from neck (7.5a) to eyes (7.5b) and finally to a description of her head (7.6). Height is an important dimension of the *wasf*.

The first indication of height is the comparison of her neck to an ivory tower (7.5a). It is also present in the description of her nose which is likened to a tower of Lebanon, overlooking Damascus (7.5de). The *wasf* reaches its term in the description of her head and then her hair (7.6). The image chosen to characterize the relationship between her head and the rest of her body (7.6a) is that of Mount Carmel, which magnificently dominates the Mediterranean Sea and the Jezreel Valley.

The ascent which takes place in the course of the *wasf* is mirrored by an ever increasing emotional intensity, which reaches its term when the king ironically yet inevitably falls for the singer of the song (7.6c). He, the king, is rendered helpless at the sight of the locks which fall from her head. The word *dallat*, 'a lock of hair', has been carefully chosen to emphasize her position of superiority. The noun derives from the verb *dlh*, 'to fall'.

From the above survey several conclusions emerge as to the functions of the imagery.

Regal imagery becomes the focus of the courtly images; oils and spices, gemstones and precious metals, even architectural and topographical details tend to gravitate around this key courtly image. The daughters of Jerusalem too are drawn in to this same sphere of influence by their belonging to a courtly milieu which naturally finds its focus in the personage of the king. An important element of narrativity moreover characterizes these regal images, contributing considerably to the dynamic of the Song. Indeed architectural details, images of monumentality, also echo this narrative movement.

Closely related to this imaginative field is the imagery of artisanship, focusing particularly upon the jewels and precious metals. Primarily visual, this imagery is evocative of the splendour of the lovers. There is, however, a marked intensification in the use of the imagery, in accordance with the movement described above, for, if in 1.10-11 there is a description of her jewellery, in 7.1 she herself is a work of art. Similarly, if in 3.6-10 there is a lengthy description of Solomon's litter which metaphorically refers to his magnificence, in 5.11-15 he himself is monumental, his arms rods of gold set with jewels (5.14), his legs alabaster columns upon bases of gold (5.15) and so on.

The language of oils and spices is an important bridge between natural and courtly imagery, for the scents which perfume the garden and vineyard are part of the same range of fragrances which the lovers enjoy indoors. Indeed, it is the particular power of fragrance to call up a place or person which results in the blurring of distinctions between past and present, inside and outside, longing and fulfilment, absence and presence. Thanks to the teasing transformations performed by this kind of imagery we lose our place in time and space and enter into a heart dialogue in which the lovers, absent or present, never cease to be one. In this respect the imagery is an important constituent in the psychological unity of the Song.

The short section entitled *Veils and Mantles*, in which I discuss the image of the veil, draws attention to a minor motif which nevertheless is constant throughout the Song, namely that of the hiddenness of the woman. Her veil, which highlights the loveliness of her eyes in 4.3 and which barely conceals her ruddy cheeks in 6.7, joins with those interiors (2.9; 5.2) which kindle yet further the man's desire. The motif of the cloak or mantle, on the other hand, is primarily a dramatic device, proper to the narrative of 5.2-8.

Finally, the daughters of Jerusalem also belong to this courtly canvas, yet primarily in a representative capacity, as the means by which the relationship is externalized and the poet freed to meditate upon the nature of love. To them also is issued the warning that love is not to be meddled with, revealing a didactic side to the Song, also characteristic of sapiential tradition. If Proverbs sets out instructions for sons (1.8, 10; 2.1; 3.1, 11, 21; 4.1, 10, 20; 5.1, 7; 6.1, 20; 7.1, 24 and so on), here it is the guidance of Israel's daughters which is the poet's chief concern. This slender evidence is perhaps not sufficient to argue for female authorship. It does however confirm the strongly feminine bias of the Song.

Chapter 2

IMAGERY OF FAMILY LIFE

Images of Motherhood

The mothers of both lovers are mentioned at various points throughout the Song, yet they never occupy anything but a secondary role as the bearers and supporters of their children. They themselves are shadowy figures, whose characters are not even sketchily developed.

The woman's mother is the first relative to be mentioned in the Song (1.6c). It is therefore with her that the survey should begin.

The woman's mother does not herself enter into the dialogue at this point, but it is by reference to her that the heroine of the Song relates to her brothers in such a way as to distance them. By referring to them as 'my mother's sons' (1.6e), she suggests that it is only by virtue of their common mother that the siblings have anything to do with each other at all. The context of this phrase elsewhere in the Old Testament confirms this intention, for on every occasion it is used to parallel the more direct term 'brothers' (Gen. 27.29; 43.29; Ps. 50.20; 69.8). At Ugarit too, the phrase 'my mother's sons' parallels the phrase 'my own brothers' (*KTU* 1.6 vi.10-11).

It is this conflict within the family which sows the seeds of her rejection by society at large. Because of her negative relationship with her brothers, she is obliged to justify herself before the daughters of Jerusalem (1.5). Home, as represented by her brothers, and society, as represented by the daughters of Jerusalem, seem to constitute a united front against her. It is only her mother with whom there seems to be the possibility of a more positive relationship.

In 6.8 the woman is again singled out, though this time not for scorn but for praise. If she was shunned by the daughters of Jerusalem in 1.6, in 6.9 she receives the admiration of the queens, concubines and young women of the court. The vocabulary used of their reaction to the woman closely resembles that used of the ideal wife in Prov. 31.28.

> Her children rise up and call her blessed
> her husband also and he praises her.

If the heroine of the Song receives the praise of the women of the court in 6.9, this admiration arises spontaneously from her lover's declaration of her incomparability:

> There may be sixty queens and eighty concubines
> and innumerable young women,
> but one alone is my dove, my perfect one...

She is neither queen nor concubine but simply the daughter of an anonymous, undistinguished mother. This relationship alone distinguishes her. Moreover, just as her lover prefers her to all the women of the court, so her mother prefers her above all her children. In 6.9c she is described as

> ...her mother's only one,
> the favourite of her who bore her.

Lover and mother are of the same opinion. His darling is her darling also. In moments of joy as in times of opposition, her mother is their closest ally.

Her mother's house (3.4; 8.2) is also the place of security *par excellence*. In contrast to the city streets, in which the lovers meet with hostility, disapprobation and even violence, her mother's house is a safe, private place, impervious to public censorship. Indeed, unlike any other lovers' place, it is free from the strictures which would make either of the lovers apprehensive. There is not, in this context, any mention of the need for her lover to flee (cf. 2.17; 4.6; 8.14).

This may be because in 3.4, as in 8.2, it is a place to which the lovers do not yet have access. The unexpected change in tense in 3.4 (*'arpennû*) suggests that the fulfilment of her desire may still belong to the future.

> I held him, now I will not let him go,
> till I bring him to my mother's house,
> to the chamber of her who conceived me.

The dramatic tension created by the shift in tense from the complete (*'aḥaztîw*) to incomplete (*'arpennû*) tense is sustained by the preposition *'ad* which links 3.4d to 3.4e by means of enjambement. It is heightened by the adjuration addressed to the daughters of Jerusalem (3.5). It closes the scene without resolving the question of whether the reunion does in fact take place in the mother's house or not.

The importance of the mother's house as a place of refuge for the lovers is conveyed by the increasingly diminutive surroundings in which the lovers find themselves. The woman's passage from the open streets (3.2) to her mother's house (3.4d) and bedchamber (3.4e) creates the impression of a series of enclosures which progressively distance the lovers from the external world. In addition, the alliterative sequence *r*, *h*, *ḥ*, which characterizes 3.4e, conveys an atmosphere which is increasingly dreamlike. 3.4e is also shorter than its counterpart 3.4d, thereby bringing the sequence quickly to a close.

The woman's mother is alluded to in each element of the parallelism. Her home constitutes the woman's home (3.4d)[1] and her room recalls her daughter's own origins (3.4e). Indeed there is even the hint that the woman's mother herself creates a third and final element in the sequence of increasingly enclosed spaces. She is referred to as 'she who conceived me' (3.4e), calling to mind her daughter's first home, the womb.

In 8.1 a similar sequence presents itself. Overburdened by public censorship, the woman wishes her lover were 'like a brother' to her. Then she could kiss him in public and take him home.[2] There is however a linguistic difficulty in the verse, namely that of how to translate *t^e lamm^e denî*, for it may be rendered 'you will teach me' (Delitzsch, Keel, Murphy) or 'she will teach me' (Falk, KJV). Alternatively, Pope and Fox suggest that one should omit the *mem* to read *tildenî* in order to parallel 3.4 (*hôratî*) more closely.[3] This last suggestion is the most satisfactory, since in 3.4 and in 8.5 there seems to be a connection in the woman's mind between the events of love and the lover's origins; in 3.4 she looks forward to being alone with her lover in the very place of her own conception as if continuity of place matters. Similarly, in 8.5, the woman precedes her declaration of love's power (8.6-8) with the memory of pain and sorrow which accompany her lover's birth. The psychoanalyst might suggest that the motif discloses the impulse to be present at one's own conception. The poet uses it to suggest that love itself constitutes a kind of birth which is repeated in every generation.

1. Cf. Gen. 24.28; Ruth 1.8.
2. Patai (1959: 196-97) interprets the verse with reference to the Koran (4.23) which states that children suckled at the same breast, that is milk siblings, may not marry each other. Unable to marry, they are free from the rules of avoidance which restrict other young men and women and may visit each other as they please, hence the expression 'like a brother' here.
3. LXX and S repeat the phrasing of 3.4.

His mother, like hers, plays a significant yet subordinate role. In 3.11 she crowns her son on his wedding day. As Keel (1986: 128) and Murphy (1990: 152) point out, there is no evidence of such a tradition in ancient Israel.[4] Neither is there any hint of crown or wedding garland in Isa. 61.10 or Ps. 45.3-9, both of which speak of a variety of ceremonial dress worn at weddings. The scene is simply a poetic flourish, a literary fiction in favour of the male lover who is temporarily identified with King Solomon. The wedding festivities, in which his mother participates and to which the daughters of Jerusalem are summoned, all pay tribute to him.

His mother is mentioned for a second and last time in 8.5. One of the difficulties of this verse is the translation of *hibbᵉlatka* and *hibbᵉlâ*, for the root may mean either 'conceive' or 'travail'. To opt for the former is to understand the woman to mean that she wakens her lover in the very place where he was conceived. In that case we are reminded of 3.5 in which her mother's house is described as the 'chamber of her who conceived me'. Alternatively, the context of the verse may suggest that the more common meaning 'travail' should be adopted, in view of the climactic statement concerning the power of love to conquer death which follows immediately afterwards (8.6). The willingness of a mother to suffer in order that her child might live is a fine example of love's triumph over death indeed. It is the second option that has been chosen in my translation.

The role of both mothers may now be summarized. As previously suggested, both mothers are present throughout the Song although neither is developed as a character in her own right. They remain anonymous, secondary figures, associated above all with the lovers' conception (3.4) and birth (8.2, 5) and with key moments in their emotional life. His mother participates in a literary fiction which celebrates his splendour and which marks the transition from adolescence to manhood (3.11), while her mother offers her home as a place of security for the lovers, a place of freedom where they may consummate their love (3.4, 8.2). Both mothers represent parental authority (1.6, 3.11) yet both are moved principally by the desires of their children's hearts. As such they are similar to mothers throughout the ancient Near East. In

---

4. The stories concerning Bathsheba (1 Kgs 1.11-31; 2.13-25), Jezebel (2 Kgs 10.13) and Athaliah (2 Kgs 11) suggest, however, that the queen mother enjoyed considerable power, particularly in Judah.

the love songs of Egypt and Sumer, as in Israel, they are associated primarily with the heart.[5]

Landy (1983: 73) has drawn attention to the contribution of infancy to adult sexuality, hence the imagery of suckling which characterizes much of the language of lovemaking. While Landy is at pains to stretch the theory as far as possible, it does seem likely that images of suckling underlie the language of eating and drinking which describes their love-making. In 8.2c for example, the woman promises to give her lover spiced wine. She then offers him the juice of her pomegranates (8.2d). The first person personal pronominal suffix of *rimmonî* strongly suggests that the reference is metaphorical, that she is in fact offering him her breasts. There may also be an echo of suckling in the extended metaphors of 4.5 and 7.8-9.[6] These images will be discussed in the sections *Vines and Vineyards* and *Animals and Birds* respectively.

Images of Fatherhood

The absence of any reference to a father-figure is indeed surprising. It is perhaps related to the fact that the Song is not so much concerned with the economic and social consequences of marriage for particular families[7] as with the exploration of the transforming power of love in the lives of individuals. Hence, in accordance with ancient Near Eastern tradition, it is the mother rather than the father who has pride of place in the exploration of romantic love. The absence of a father figure does however also consolidate the feminine bias of the Song.

5. For example, in the Egyptian love song:

Mother is good in commanding me thus;
avoid seeing <him>! (Fox 1985: 52)

Or in the Sumerian love song:

Inanna, at the command of her mother, Bathed,
anointed herself with goodly oil,
Covered her body with the noble *pala*-garment,
Took [...] her dowry,
Arranged the lapis lazuli about (her) neck,
Grasped her seal Min in her hand (*ANET*: 639)

6. Further images of suckling are afforded by the LXX which consistently translates *dôdîm* as 'breasts' rather than as 'lovemaking' (1.2; 4.10).

7. *KTU* 1.24 describes how the moon god Yarikhu acquired his bride Nikkalu. Explicit reference is made to the bride's father in connection with the bride-price (*KTU* 1.24 20-24).

Sibling Relationships

The form of address 'my sister, my bride' appears several times in one section only (4.9–5.1). This section corresponds to what will be argued in *The Garden* to be the climax and midpoint of the Song. There, by means of the image of the garden, the woman becomes a figure of paradise for her lover. She is both the place and means of his return.

The epithets 'my sister, my bride' are skilfully employed in 4.9–5.1. Initially (4.9a, 10a, 12a) the epithets are situated at the end of the first colon, thereby underlining and isolating what precedes. The element isolated by the epithets is invariably picked up in some way in the second colon although the relationship between the repeated elements becomes more complex as the sequence develops. In 4.9 it is the verbal form *libbabtinî* that is isolated by the epithet. In 4.10 it is the noun *dodayik*. In 4.12 there is repetition and variation, *gan na'ûl* becomes *gal na'ûl*. The effect of the epithets on each occasion is to slow down the description, and to communicate the delicate process by means of which the garden opens to welcome her lover. In 5.1, when her lover at last accepts the woman's invitation to come and eat, the relationship of the epithet to the verse is quite different. There, every element is new so as to convey his haste:

> I have come to my garden, my sister and bride,
> I have gathered my myrrh and my spices,
> I have eaten my honeycomb with my honey,
> and drunk my wine with my milk.

To address the woman as 'my sister' is not peculiar to the Song. It is evident in Sumerian sacred marriage songs[8] and even more frequently in the love songs of Egypt.[9] It is also used by Anat of her relationship with her intended, Aghat (*KTU* 1.18.24), and by Baal of his wife Anat (*KTU* 1.3 iv.39).

Patai (1959: 16) points out that in biblical narrative the most suitable wife for a Hebrew patriarch was thought to be his sister even though such a marriage would have been unacceptable in real life. Indeed the marriage of siblings is implicit in the stories concerning the origins of the world (Gen. 4–5) and the perpetuation of the human race after the flood

---

8.   The poem entitled 'Set me free, my sister' includes both 'brother' and 'sister' epithets (*ANET*: 645).

9.   See Fox (1985: 13).

(Gen. 10). It is a source of irony in Gen. 12.10-16 and 20.12-18 where Abraham presents his wife Sarah as his sister in order to save his own skin. In the Song, however, the ties of kinship have simply become a metaphor for love. The epithet 'my sister' declares the man's wonder before this woman who, though a stranger, seems always to have been known to him. She is at once *'ahôt*, his sister (4.9, 10, 12; 5.1, 2), and the woman of his choice, *kala* (4.9, 10, 12; 5.1), his bride. Likewise he is to her both *'ah*, 'brother' (8.1), *dôd*, 'lover' (1.13, 14, 16; 2.3, 8, 9, 10, 16; 4.16; 5.4, 5, 6, 10, 16; 6.2, 3 and so on) and *re'*, 'friend' (5.16).

Not only does he claim that she is unique (6.9) but he stresses the harmony of her form. The language of twinship is particularly evocative in this respect. Twice, and in almost identical terms, the woman's perfectly formed, glistening white teeth are compared to ewes and their young as they come up out of the water (4.2ab; 6.6). Each ewe bears twins, *mat'îmôt* (4.2c; 6.6c), the very form of which draws attention to duality on account of the repetition, in the same order, of the letters *mem* and *taw*. In addition, the adjective *šakkulâ*, 'bereaved', in 4.2d echoes *šekkullam*, 'all of which' in the preceding colon (4.2c).

The scarlet thread which marks the meeting of her lips (4.3a) and the pomegranate halves[10] which characterize her rosy cheeks (4.3c) both depend upon the notion of division to emphasize duality (4.2). In addition, the ordinal number *šenî*, 'two' (4.5a), echoes *šanî*, 'scarlet' (4.3a). Both recall the metaphor of her teeth, *šinnayik*, with which the theme of duality began.

The motif of twinship characterizes her breasts which are compared to two fawns, the twins of a gazelle (4.5; 7.4). The expression is the same in both chapters, except that it is elaborated in 4.5 by an evocation of the delight her lover takes in them (4.5c). As suggested above, a strange reversal has taken place, for her suckling breasts themselves now suck. The twinship motif is emphasized by the adjective *šenî* on both occasions (4.5a; 7.4a).

The language of twinship expresses the perfection of her form, just as the language of kinship expresses the close bond forged between the lovers. The woman's relationship with her own brothers however is less ideal. While she wishes her lover were her milk brother (8.1), enabling

10. *pelah* may either designate a slice or cut of something, for example a fig cake (1 Sam. 30.12) or each of two halves (Judg. 9.53; 2 Sam. 11.21). Given the emphasis upon duality in this verse, it is the latter option that has been chosen here. JB and NIV are also of this opinion.

her to enjoy his company freely, her relationship with her own brothers is very bad. It is against this backcloth that the language of kinship is set.

The woman's brothers appear in a very poor light in 1.6, angry with her for some reason which is not disclosed. In this verse, the activity proper to one subject is applied metaphorically to the next in sequence. Thus it is that the sun (1.6b), like the daughters of Jerusalem (1.6a), metaphorically glances (1.6b) and that her brothers (1.6c), like the sun (1.6b), metaphorically burn (1.6c). A close relationship linguistically between the sun which has scorched her, the stares of the daughters of Jerusalem and the anger of her brothers makes this cohesion possible.[11] As Landy (1983: 148) has again suggested, however, this relationship fails to disclose the solution to the enigma, rather it intensifies the puzzle.

The responsibility for her blackness, which is evidently the source of her discomfort, seems to be laid squarely on her brothers' shoulders. They are the ones who imposed upon her the heavy manual labour which has so damaged her complexion. The foreshortening which takes place in 1.6e, the result of which is to identify the vineyard with her very self, alters our perspective to such a degree as to make us wonder whether her brothers' imposition of such a task was not in response to the violation of some moral norm from which they sought in vain to protect her. Is it the family honour which is at stake and which arouses their sudden indignation? The issue is perhaps that of a suitor and the precociousness of a young sister who has already made her choice for herself. It must be remembered that in the ancient Near East love and marriage were not the concern primarily of individuals but of families who settled between themselves the important economic question of the bride-price. Such a transaction was dependent upon the assurance of her purity. In such a context the brothers' indignation is easily understood.

The heroine of the Song, however, sees things from a radically different perspective, for she is consumed by a love which is of absolute value in itself and which defies the intrusion of economic concerns (8.7). Indeed

11. The woman begs the daughters of Jerusalem not to 'look' at her (*r'h*) because the sun has 'glanced' at her (*šzp*), that is, burnt her. The verb *šzp* literally means 'to see' (cf. Job 20.9; 28.7). A similar root *šdp* however means 'to burn' (Gen. 41.6, 23, 27). Given the interchangeability of *z* and *d* in Aramaic, it is easy to understand how a play on words is possible; the metaphorical reading of *šzp* is reinforced by a linguistic transformation which underlines the relationship between the two terms. It is however the brothers who are chiefly responsible for her plight; if the sun has scorched her, it is because their anger has 'burned' against her first. A second play on words comes into view, for the verb *ḥrh* may mean 'to burn' or 'to be angry'.

she spurns all those who seek to offer money for love. Love, as she has experienced it, is totally free (8.11-12).

Her suffering is intensified by the fact that her brothers are more numerous than she and seem to be able to exercise more pressure on her due to their sheer number.[12] This is all the more galling given that they are her siblings, the representatives only of an absent paternal authority. Their repressive behaviour, as she interprets it, is echoed in the nightwatchmen who, in like manner, use their strength and number to abuse her (5.7).[13] Like her brothers, they are anonymous and undifferentiated, incapable of any personal relationship with her. Moreover their negative attitude towards her sows the seeds of suspicion in the daughters of Jerusalem, before whom she is also made to feel alone and vulnerable (1.5).

The brothers henceforth retreat from the scene to reappear implicitly in 8.8, in words originally spoken by themselves but now quoted with great immediacy by the heroine of the Song, their little sister. She recalls the time when, before she had even reached maturity, they began to voice their concern as regards her forthcoming marriage. The tone however is no longer that of intense emotion but that of playful banter by means of which she enters into their speculation for a moment, only to denounce it.

Song 8.8 asks a question to which her brothers make an inappropriate response (8.9), for rather than allow their little sister to mature into responsible womanhood, they plan to adorn her with a silver turret or board her up with planks of cedar, depending on how she seems to be turning out. These images, describing their overprotectiveness towards her, remain enigmatic, for the reader is given no clue as to whether the *waw* of 8.8c connecting the door and the wall is adversative or complementary, whether to be one or the other is of greater value and according to what criterion. We only know—later—that the heroine of the Song is a wall and is proud to be so (8.10).

Let us press the images a little more closely; we shall soon see their impenetrability. Not only is the *waw* of 8.9c ambiguous but so also is the use of the verb *sûr* which may mean either 'to adorn', 'fashion' or 'besiege'. If understood according to the first of these possibilities, the form *naṣûr* parallels *nibneh*, 'we will build'. This would suggest that the

---

12. No indication of their precise number is given. They are referred to simply in the plural as *bᵉne 'mmî*, 'my mother's sons' (1.6c).

13. They are referred to simply as the *haššomᵉrîm*, the 'keepers' (5.7a).

images of door and wall are complimentary, denoting two kinds of beauty or of temperament, the one rather more introverted and reserved than the other (Landy 1983: 160-61). According to this interpretation, silver and cedar are used in celebration of her beauty. If, on the other hand, we understand the verb to imply some kind of imposed enclosure, wall and door are best considered to be antithetical, the door representing moral weakness and the wall, chastity. Her brothers therefore promise to react accordingly, rewarding her for her chastity and imposing severe restrictions upon her if she fails to observe their norms. In the light of their negative attitude to her in 1.6 and the vigor, of her reply in 8.10 in which she asserts her independence, the latter interpretation is perhaps more characteristic.

The ambivalence of the text however is surely well calculated, for in the light of the peace and well-being she finds in her lover in 8.10, the brothers' opinion is of little account. Indeed it is the inappropriateness of their designs to which she objects. In stark response, therefore, to their designation of her as a little sister without breasts, she now proudly announces that, fully nubile, her breasts are like towers. The image of the wall similarly works in her favour, complementing those images of fountain and garden (4.12), which open to her lover alone. On the basis of the association in 8.10 between the woman's breasts and towers, Landy (1983: 162) concludes that the wall refers to her torso and the door to her genitalia. This however is more than the poet is willing to specify.

Imagery drawn from family life falls into two main categories, namely images referring to motherhood and those concerning sibling relationships. Mothers and brothers remain shadowy figures, anonymous and undifferentiated, important only in their relationship to the lovers. In this respect the woman's mother is their closest ally, protecting the lovers and offering them the shelter of her house. Her brothers, on the other hand, are a negative oppressive influence, from which the woman progressively escapes. Indeed, the story of love's triumph unfolds in the context of their opposition.

Not only is the man's family yet more shadowy, but only his mother is mentioned. Each of these elements, along with that of the absence of any paternal figure, contribute to the strongly feminine bias of the Song; it is the woman and her family who predominate, and within this group it is her mother who has the greatest positive influence.

Mother and brothers are also internalized in the images of motherhood and of kinship which express different aspects of their relationship. He comes to suckle at her breasts, to feed on her, she who is his sister and the one with whom he senses the closest possible kinship. Images of twinship also contribute to this desire for ever deeper unity. It is in his description of her breasts and cheeks that he reveals his deepest desire.

Chapter 3

NATURE IMAGERY

Flowers, Fruit and Trees

Flowers are most often used in the Old Testament to evoke the transitory
nature of human life (Ps. 103.15; Job 14.2; Isa. 28.1; 40.6, 7, 8). In the
Song they are associated with the invitation to the lovers to recognize
that spring has come and that the time of love is near.

The first appearance of this theme is in 2.12-13 where the arrival of
spring flowers[1] is associated with the call of the dove, with the appearance of newly formed figs[2] and blossom on the fragrant vines.[3] The
theme reappears in 6.11 and in 7.12.

It is not coincidental that the union of the lovers is described in terms
of a variation of these images—the ripened grapes, harvested, and
already made into wine, are frequently an image of lovemaking (1.2;
4.10) and the ripened grape is on at least one occasion an image of the
breasts for which he longs (7.9). An orchard of pomegranates (4.13)
awaits the lover who comes to his lover's garden to delight in her, and
ripened fruits over her door are a token of their intimacy within (7.13).
The difference is only in the maturity of the ripening process—the
progress of the season maps the climate of their love.

The fruits which bedeck the lovers' door (7.14b) are accompanied by

1. *niṣṣanîm* is a *hapax legomenon* in the Old Testament. The noun is usually
found in the singular, either in the masculine (Gen. 40.10) or in the feminine
(Isa. 18.5; Job. 15.33). The root *nṣṣ* is related to brightness (cf. Ezek. 1.7). Here it is
used to evoke the dazzling sight of a carpet of spring flowers.

2. *pageha*, translated 'its figs', is a *hapax legomenon*. In the context it refers to
the first unripe fruit of the fig tree. The accompanying verb *hattᵉ'enâ* is a rare word,
used only in Gen. 50.2, 6 where it is used in the sense of 'embalming'. Here, it has
the sense of 'ripening'.

3. *sᵉmadar* has been translated as an attributive accusative, 'the vines being in
bloom'. The word is unique to the Song (2.15c; 7.13c).

the scent of mandrakes (7.14a); together they announce joyfully that indeed the time for love has come. The appearance of mandrakes (*haddûda'îm*) in the place where she promises to give her lover (*dôdî*) her love (*doday*) stresses the congruence between the processes of nature and the events of love. The play on the root *dôd*, meaning 'lover', 'mandrake' and 'lovemaking', reinforces the associations with fertility which the plant enjoyed throughout the ancient world.[4] In particular, it is reminiscent of the story recounted in Gen. 30.14-16 in which Leah conceives and bears a son to Jacob thanks to the mandrakes gathered for her.

The flowers most frequently mentioned in the Song are the *šôšannîm* (2.1; 4.5; 5.13; 6.2; 7.2), the identity of which is debatable. On the basis of LXX's rendering *krinon*, and Vg *lilium*, the flower has traditionally been associated with the *lilium candidum* or madonna lily, a flower proved to be native to Palestine (Möldenke 1952: 164). As such it is an image of great delicacy, evocative of the woman's purity and simplicity.

Another possibility is that the flower belongs to the *nymphae* or water-lily family and that the form *šôšanna* is a loanword borrowed from the Egyptian *sššn* or *sšn*, 'lotus' (Tournay 1988: 58). Herodotus (Legrand 1936: 125) is a help here, for he writes c. 430 BCE that what is known in the Greek world as a lily is called a lotus in Egypt. This explains why the LXX read the word as it did.

Although the Egyptian water-lily, the lotus, is not native to Palestine, there is evidence that the *nymphea alba*, the white water-lily, or the *nymphea caericula*, the blue water-lily, did grow there (Möldenke 1952: 154-55). Moreover the Egyptian water-lily, the *nymphea lotus*, would have been known, if not in its natural habitat, then by means of artistic representation, for as Pope suggests (1977: 368), the motif appears on Egyptian, Canaanite and even Solomonic artifacts.[5] The Egyptian love

4. On an Egyptian wall painting, dated c. 1340, an Egyptian queen is depicted holding two mandrakes and a lotus bud to her husband's nose (Keel 1986: 239). Her open dress is suggestive of her amorous intentions. Moreover, the motif is a common-place in Egyptian love poetry (Fox 1985: 8, 9, 12, 31). In the Greek world, the mandrake was an epithet of Aphrodite (Pope 1977: 648). At Ugarit too, the plant is associated with love although the exact significance of putting the plant into the ground (*KTU* 1.3 iv 24, 30) is a matter of debate. According to De Moor (1987: 9) it is a gesture in favour of peace. According to Gibson (1977: 51) the gesture was in favour of bringing rain to water earth.

5. Pope (1977: 368) draws attention to the presence of the motif on Canaanite Astarte plaques. Keel (1986: 80) presents drawings of goblets in the shape of lotus

poets too draw on this motif (Fox 1985: 9, 12, 32).

With this second option, the balance of the imagery is altered significantly, for the water-lily implies the presence of water wherever the flower appears. It implies that the valleys of 2.1 are river valleys, that the fawns feeding on water-lilies in 4.5 are feeding by the water's edge and that the water-lilies growing in the garden (6.2) are dependent upon pools or irrigation canals.

Each of these images is in some way appropriate to the woman: she is a water-lily growing quietly by the river bank, shrouded by thorns and thistles (2.1), she is the one whose breasts suggest the luxuriant water-lilies on which favoured fawns may feed[6] (4.5), she is the garden to which her lover goes down to gather water-lilies (6.2), a metaphor for her special charms.[7] The implicit presence of water on each of these occasions is entirely appropriate, for she is not only a 'locked garden' (4.12) but also a 'fountain sealed' (4.12), a garden fountain (4.15), a well of living water (4.15).

The association of the flower with water also helps make sense of 5.13. There, her lover's lips are likened to lilies which distil liquid myrrh. The image is of the spreading petals of the water-lily. They mirror the mouth-watering nature of his anticipation. The liquid myrrh which falls from these water-lilies is inspired by the water in which the plants grow. There is no such ready an explanation as regards the madonna lily.

There is one other flower mentioned in the Song, namely the *habasṣelet*, the exact nature of which is unknown. It appears elsewhere only once, namely Isa. 35.1. LXX and Vg are non-committal in their translation, using only the generic terms *anthos* and *flos*. The Targum is a little more decisive and translates 'narcissus'. Möldenke (1952: 234) agrees that the form most likely does describe some sort of bulb— crocus, an asphodel, a hyacinth or narcissus. Following LXX and Vg,

---

flowers, found in Egypt and Palestine. He also depicts (1986: 109) a Meggido ivory in which a Canaanite warrior king is handed a lotus flower by his lady. As regards Israel, he agrees with Möldenke (1952: 154) that the Phoenician artists who worked on the temple designed capitals inspired by lotus flowers (1 Kgs 7.19, 22, 26).

6.   Herodotus (2.92, see Legrand 1936: 125) also testifies to the edibility of various parts of the water-lily. According to him the root of the lotus is sweet to the taste and the seeds of the water-lily may be eaten fresh or dried.

7.   Tournay (1988: 58) points to Egyptian paintings which depict the harvesting of lotuses. He also draws attention to the erotic associations of going to the marshes to gather papyrus; in 'The Story of Herdsman', a woman tries to seduce a shepherd by a papyrus marsh.

however, I have simply translated the word by 'flower' on the grounds that the point the woman is making in 2.1 is that she is indistinguishable from the other flowers of the field. Her lover however turns her modesty to highest praise; you, he responds, outshine all your peers, as a water-lily far surpasses in beauty the briars and thorns which surround it (2.2).[8]

With these words, she models her praise of him upon his praise of her; as an apple tree surpasses all the trees of the wood, so her lover is beyond compare vis-à-vis other young men (2.3).[9] The sturdy apple tree henceforth becomes an appropriate image for her lover who, with masculine chivalry and with fatherly tenderness, shelters his young bride (2.3cd). At this point, however, the simile of 2.1-2 is replaced by a metaphor which leaves the object of the image of the fruit undeclared. The sweetness of the fruit of the tree is presumably a modest reference to the tenderness of the youth's embrace (2.3d).

The imagery of flowers and trees which describes first her modesty (2.1) and then his chivalry (2.3) parallels and reverses that of 1.13-14 in which she shelters her lover in her arms; he is to her a spray of henna blossom, its fragrant flowers are held in her embrace. Usually it is she who, on account of her delicate, feminine beauty, is likened to a flower. In 1.13-14, however, the roles are reversed.

The apples which bring her such joy in 2.3 are the very fruits she later longs for, in order to heal the wound of his absence. In her great yearning for him, raisin cakes[10] and apples act as a substitute for what food and drink can never provide (2.5).

Apples are also used by the lover in the context of longing. In 7.9 the scent of her breath is likened to the fragrance of apples. This fragrance is

8. 'Water-lily' has been exceptionally shortened to 'lily' in order to avoid too cumbersome a rendering in this swift dialogue between the lovers (2.1-3).

9. A decision also had to be made as to the identification of *tappûaḥ*. Its etymology is *nph*, 'to breathe', suggesting a fragrant fruit. Möldenke (1952: 184-85) argues for the *prunus armeniaca*, the 'apricot tree', on the grounds that the tree is native to Palestine and that its fruit is sweet and fragrant. It therefore satisfies all the requirements of the imagery of the Song (2.3, 5; 7.9). The traditional rendering, 'apple' (KJV, RSV), is however preferable since the form clearly means 'apple' in Mishnaic Hebrew (see Jastrow 1921). Keel (1986: 92) points out that a quantity of charred apples have been found at Sinai.

10. These cakes or biscuits probably consisted of dried, pressed grapes. They are associated with the fertility cult in Hos. 1.3 but not in 2 Sam. 6.19 or 1 Chron. 16.3.

but a prelude, however, to the kisses which he anticipates and which he compares to a good wine.

The motif of the apple tree appears for the last time in 8.5c. Whereas 8.5ab is probably uttered by the daughters of Jerusalem, 8.5c seems to be spoken by the woman.[11] The image recalls that of 2.12. There, the male lover is likened to an apple tree which shelters her and gives her its fruit. In 8.5, he takes her place under the apple tree and as he lies in its shade, she comes to awaken him.

The use of the verb *'wr* in this verse reminds the reader of those adjurations in which the woman pleads with the daughters of Jerusalem not to arouse love prematurely (2.7; 3.5; 8.4). There, the subject was the abstract noun 'love' and the verb was translated by 'to arouse' or 'stir up'. Here however the subject is her lover, hence one is more inclined to translate the same verb *'wr* by 'awake'. The convergence of the verb *'wr* with the motif of the apple tree may suggest that this awakening has erotic overtones, for the verb is used of her invitation to her lover in 4.16 and the motif of the apple tree appears in connection with her lover's 'fruit' in 2.3.

It is also unclear to what event she refers. Does she refer to the relatively recent past, to an occasion on which she awoke him under an apple tree which was coincidentally also the place of his birth? Or is the awakening to which she refers the birth itself? The parallelism of 8.5de seems to point the reader in this direction, hinting that he was destined for her love from the start. This same sentiment is expressed in a Sumerian love song translated by Alster (1985: 154):

> My (own mother) gave birth to me for your sake,
> My...gave birth to me for your sake.

The imagery is complicated further by reference to the man's mother who not only bore him (8.5d) but perhaps also conceived him there (8.5a). The uncertainty relates to the translation of the verbs *ḥibbᵉlatᵉka* and *ḥibbᵉlâ*. They were discussed in the section entitled *Motherhood*.

One last ambiguity concerns the tree itself, for the definite article may refer to a particular tree of which the reader is intended to know something. There are many instances in the Old Testament however where the definite article is best translated by the indefinite article (Gibson 1994: 115). The suggestion of a particular tree lends itself to symbolic

---

11. LXX prefers to limit her initiative. Contrary to the vocalization of the MT, it attributes 8.5b to her lover.

interpretation and to the discernment of echoes of stories concerning trees in the mythology of the ancient Near East. In particular, the motif is reminiscent of the tree of life of the Gilgamesh story and of Genesis 2–3.

Even if the woman's words do have a certain timelessness which allows something of the ancient myths to shine through, these echoes are nevertheless subordinate to the lovers' very particular, personal story. The reference to her lover's birth under the tree and her identification with his mother's pain is primarily a way of pledging her love to him. It is also a way of acknowledging that suffering is part of love. As suggested in the section on *Motherhood*, this is a fitting prelude to the declaration of love's power in the following verse (8.6).

Not only apples, but pomegranates too have a place in the Song. On account of the multiplicity of their seeds, they were long considered to be a symbol of fertility and a sign of life in the ancient Near East.[12] It is not surprising therefore that they were to be seen decorating the pillars of the temple (2 Chron. 3.16; 4.13) and were embroidered upon the skirts of the priestly robes (Exod. 39.25). Moreover they grew in abundance in the Levant, as is evident in the place-name Rimmon (Josh. 15.32; Zech. 14.10) which derives from the fruit.

Pomegranate blossom is sought in 6.11 as a sign of the arrival of spring and as confirmation in the external world of the timeliness of love. In 4.3 and 6.7 pomegranates appear in descriptive songs about the woman. In both, the open pomegranate is the simile used to describe her rosy cheeks as seen through her veil. Though the images are identical, the context is slightly different. In 4.3 the image follows the description of her lips, whereas in 6.7 the image follows directly upon the description of her teeth. The impression is however of sequences which mirror each other. This is partly due to the fact that previous to the description of her lips in 4.3 is a description of her teeth almost identical to that of 6.6. The slight element of differentiation does not disrupt the harmony of the whole. Rather, it enhances it.

Between these two identical images is the extended image of the garden (4.12–5.1). There, image and referent are drawn so closely together that, for a time, the woman is described in terms of botanical imagery without the mediation of prepositions such as 'like' or 'as'

---

12. Keel (1986: 134 fig. 76) draws attention to the pomegranate trees which flank the mountain god from whose holy mountain the four rivers flow in the thirteenth-century Assyrian ivory from Assur. The ensemble is evocative of paradise.

which would otherwise alert us to the presence of a simile. Indeed the absence of any direct comparison between the parts of her body and the component parts of the garden creates the impression of her diffuse presence throughout the garden. The orchard of pomegranates and the exotic trees and spices all convey her freshness, her fruitfulness, her readiness for love.

Nowhere is the ambiguity between background and foreground more keenly felt than in 8.2. There, the woman longs to bring her lover to her mother's house. There, she promises him spiced wine and the juice of her pomegranates. This pomegranate juice could refer literally to the juice of the pomegranates growing in her mother's garden. It is much more likely, however, that the pronoun 'my' indicates an allusion to her breasts.

In the course of these metaphorical transformations different aspects of the pomegranate are called upon. In 6.11 the poet is concerned with its blossom, in 4.3 and 6.7 he or she is concerned with the colour of the fruit and the arrangement of its seeds and fleshy particles, in 4.13 he dwells upon the abundance of the harvest and finally, in 8.2, he speaks of pomegranate juice. The consistency lent to the Song by the stability of the motif never leads to boredom. On the contrary, the ingenuity with which a single image is employed gives spontaneity to the Song.

Just as flowers are associated throughout the Song with delicacy and beauty, most often feminine beauty, and fruits with the fullness of love and the maturity of the lovers, so trees are elements of security and stability in the Song. The apple tree is an image of the lover's protective presence by the woman's side in 2.7. In the same way, the image of the palm tree in 7.6 is an image of her awesome strength. In the external world too these same characteristics are displayed; the cedars and pine trees provide a secure bower for the lovers in a world in which they are dispossessed (1.17) and the palanquin which bears King Solomon is made of wood from Lebanon (3.9), a solid and enduring material, fit for the carriage of a king.

Trees appear with greatest concentration and variety in the image of the garden (4.13-14). Moreover, reference to water both follows (4.15) and precedes (4.13a), creating the impression of an oasis of life. Remarkable is the impression of proliferation in this passage. This impression is enhanced by means of alliteration characterizing not only individual consonants but entire sequences: the sequence *p r* characterizes *pardes* (4.13a) and *pᵉrî* (4.13b), for example, the sequence *k n* is evident in *karkom kinnamôn* (4.14b) and the masculine plural ending *îm* occurs in *kᵉparîm* and *nᵉradîm*, both in 4.13c. These alliterative sequences are particularly effective where, as in the last two examples, the words are in apposition, forming an alliterative pair.

The effect of alliteration changes as the description proceeds. In 4.13c-14b the rather harsh palatals *kaph* and *qoph* predominate. Then, in 4.14c-e the post-dental *lamedh* comes to the fore. This soft sound reminds the reader of how the description of the garden began, for *lamedh* is also alliterative there (4.12). The sense of abundance is also conveyed in other ways, namely by the hyperbolic repetition of the adjective *kol*, 'all' (4.14c, e) and by the juxtaposition of different species, connected either by the conjunction *waw* (4.14a, b, d) or simply by the preposition *'im*, 'with'. The image of the garden, in which these trees flourish, will be discussed in due course.

Animals and Birds

The fauna of the Song, like the flora, are highly varied. There are domestic animals, sheep and goats which are associated with a pastoral way of life. They are seen moving over the hillside in search of fresh pasture land and watercourses. There are also gazelles, hinds and young stags[13] roaming around the open countryside according to season, animals associated with the hunt and with the royal park. Wild predators, hostile to human beings, also have a place in the Song. There are lions and leopards in the heights, and little foxes who make destructive forays into the orchards of the cultivated countryside.

Some of these animals display particular characteristics which disclose something about the lovers and their relationship. In this respect they are a rich source of imagery for the descriptive songs. More often they add movement and vitality to the natural world in which the relationship grows, mirroring the lovers' struggles and their joys.

Ewes with their lambs and goats with their kids constitute the pastoral scene of 1.7-8. Even though the woman is in some tension with the scene, the image is nevertheless one of rest and repose, of harmony between human and beast; the shepherd moves with his flock, lying down with them at noon at a suitable watering place. The woman too

---

13. The noun *'oper* is peculiar to the Song (2.9, 17; 4.5; 7.4; 8.14). In post-biblical Hebrew it designates the young of an animal. In Arabic, a similar term is used of the young of the chamois or ibex (Pope 1977: 390).

participates in this general movement, for she too is depicted temporarily as a shepherdess in charge of her flock (1.8c).

Though the pastoral scene appears to fade never to return again with any consistency, an echo is to be found in the extended metaphors of 4.1-2 and 6.5-6. They describe her vivacious curls and her glistening white, perfectly regular teeth. Indeed, the metaphors used are so highly developed as to overshadow the parts of the body described. Rather than concentrate upon her hair and teeth, we become preoccupied with the beautifully balanced descent of the goats down the hillside and the ascent of the shorn ewes and their lambs up the other side.

These are, moreover, no ordinary beasts; the ewes are clean and healthy and each is flanked by two sturdy lambs, an image reminiscent of Isa. 40.11. The aim is to convey her feminine maturity and capacity for motherhood every bit as much as it is to describe her hair and teeth. Pastoral motifs have introduced another, hidden agenda.

Young deer and gazelles frequently appear in the Song, particularly in association with the woman's lover. His energetic visits to and from her door (2.8-9, 17; 8.14) recall the agility of these shy animals whose swiftness is well documented in the Old Testament (2 Sam. 2.18; 1 Chron. 12.9; Sir. 27.20; Isa. 35.6; Hab. 3.19). In Ps. 42.2 the psalmist's yearning for God is described in terms of a doe longing for 'streams of water'. The lover's longing is also the motivation of his flight to her door (2.8-9).

The motif appears for the first time in 2.9. The male lover, whose imminent arrival is announced in 2.8, progressively takes on the appearance of a gazelle, an image which fits perfectly the verbs 'to leap' (*dlg*) and 'to bound' (*qpṣ*)[14] which characterize his enthusiastic advance. The simile persists throughout the verse with the result that we see simultaneously a gentle stag and an expectant lover waiting at the woman's door (2.9c-f).[15] The tension, and likewise the ambiguity, are broken in 2.10 when, at last, he speaks. With his words, the image of the lovely gazelle immediately fades and the lover takes on once more the full

14. *qpṣ* usually has the sense of 'to shut' or 'to draw'. It is not used elsewhere meaning 'to leap' although this usage is attested in the Aramaic and Arabic cognates, *qpṣ and qfz* (Pope 1977: 389).

15. The vocabulary of this verse is unusual; *'oper* is a *hapax legomenon*, presumed to refer to a young stag. *kotlenû*, translated 'our wall', is unique to the Hebrew part of the Old Testament. *meṣîṣ*, the *hiphil* participle of *ṣûṣ*, 'to blossom', here takes on the sense of 'to gaze', paralleling *mašgîaḥ*, 'to peer'. Finally *ḥarakkîm*, paralleling *ḥallonôt*, 'windows', is a *hapax legomenon* attested later in postbiblical Hebrew.

stature of a man. His request to her to come away with him (2.10-11) is followed by her joyful declaration of their mutual belonging to one another (2.16). Her song of delight however stops short when she abruptly dismisses him to the mountains of Bether (2.17). This unexpected command parallels his spontaneous arrival over the mountains in 2.8. On both occasions he is likened to a gazelle or a young stag which moves quickly through the countryside.

A similar command marks the close of the Song (8.14). However, the effect is to assure us that the Song will never end. The lovers will evermore be engaged in love's game of hide and seek.

When the image of the gazelle is applied to the woman, it is not primarily on account of the agility of the animal but because of its grace and beauty, those same qualities which make the image of the doe appropriate in the characterization of the ideal wife in Prov. 5.19. As regards the woman of the Song, it is her youthful femininity which the young animals highlight. In 4.5 her breasts are described as 'two fawns, twins of a gazelle' for, like these animals, they are perfectly balanced, and dappled, like the fawns' coats. The maternal function of her breasts is evoked by a transformation of this imagery whereby the young fawns, which initially describe the perfection of her form, subsequently anticipate the presence of her lover at her side. The twin fawns cease to be identified with her breasts. Instead they proceed to feed on them (4.5c). With this development image and referent are less precisely related to each other than before (4.5a). Now there is no explicit association between breasts and water-lilies. This however is the conclusion to which the reader seems inevitably drawn.

It has often been said that gazelles and deer are associated with love in the ancient Near East. Keel (1986: 89-94) demonstrates this point with reference to iconography, Pope (1977: 386) with reference to Mesopotamian magical spells. Keel implies that associations with the love goddess are implicit in the Song by means of these animals which are her representatives.[16] This is especially true of the adjurations of 2.7 and 3.5 where the animals are invoked in an oath. It is likely, however, that the association in 2.7 and 3.5 is not only with love but also with speed of

---

16. Gordis (1974: 26-28) argues that the animals may also be invoked in order to avoid using the divine name. According to him, the poet replaces such customary oaths as *be'lohê ṣ^eba'ôt* or *b^e'el šadday* by a similar sounding phrase, *biṣ^eba'ôt 'ô b^e'aylôt haśśadeh*, 'by the gazelles and hinds of the fields', choosing animals which symbolize love for the substitutions.

movement and freedom; while love is dormant, the daughters of Jerusalem are as free as the gazelles and hinds of the field. Once love is awoken, all this will change.

Even as the gazelle is particularly associated with the male lover, so the dove, also traditionally associated with love,[17] is most often, though not exclusively, associated with the woman. Her eyes are likened to doves in 1.15, an image which develops and makes more precise a general declaration of her beauty in the same verse. Her dove-like eyes thereby become the focus of her loveliness.[18] The metaphor is particularly appropriate because the *î* and *n* of *'ênayik yônîm* echo sounds which are already well established in the verse. These same sounds are, moreover, taken up in her response, for she models her words of praise to her lover on his address to her (1.16a).

It has often been asked in what way her eyes resemble doves. Aquila, Peshitta and Vg understand the image to refer not to the birds themselves, but to their eyes. On the basis of Egyptian artistic convention, Gerleman (1965: 114) suggests that it is the shape of the bird that is called upon. Much more clear than the objective correspondence, however, which remains ambiguous, are the qualities of gentleness (Mt. 10.16), delicacy and liveliness which are common to tenor and to vehicle. It is these same qualities of vivacity and delicate beauty that are discovered in the man's eyes later in the Song (5.12). The simile of 5.12 far exceeds in its detail the simple metaphor of 1.15. The use of the same basic imagery, however, discloses how very deeply the two protagonists love each other; they describe each other using the same language and hence convince the reader that they are not two but one.

The initial comparison of his eyes to doves in 5.12a takes on a life of its own in subsequent colons as the poet describes how these doves sit quietly in a pool of milky foam.[19] The image is surely of a river in spate and of doves riding the foamy current. It is an image of serene steadiness amid turbulent movement, describing both the steadiness and

17. Keel (1986: 71-75) draws attention to the presence of doves in the iconography of love in the ancient Near East, associated with Ishtar/Astarte, and, in Hellenistic times, with Aphrodite. By the second half of the second century BCE, he claims, the dove had become a symbol of love throughout the entire Mediterranean.

18. It is not surprising that the woman's ability to charm is mediated by means of her eyes, for, as Murphy (1990: 159) points out, they were recognized in the Old Testament to be the vehicle of a woman's power (Prov. 6.25; Sir. 26.9).

19. *'al-mille't*, literally 'sitting in fullness', LXX renders 'sitting by the fullness of water'.

liveliness of his gaze. As with 1.16, attempts have been made to identify different parts of the lover's eyes. In particular, the reference to milk in 5.12c may encourage the reader to make an association with the whites of the eye, an image reminiscent of the Keret legend in which the eyelashes of a girl form the rim of a bowl filled with 'frothy milk' (*KTU* 1.14, iii 43). If an awareness of the whites of the eye does impose itself in 5.12, this however does not necessarily imply that the iris and pupil are also to be identified. Indeed, in someone of swarthy complexion, the whites of the eyes are probably the most prominent feature. Here, they contrast markedly with the darkness of his hair, which is 'black as a raven' (5.11c).

Apart from its beauty and vivacity, the dove is also notable for its shyness (Jer. 48.28). It is this quality which is emphasized in 2.14 where the woman is compared to a dove hiding in the cleft of the rock. It is also evident in 4.1c where shyness and discretion add to her beauty; she is beautiful, her eyes are like doves, yet they are barely visible behind her veil.[20] Her inaccessibility, alluded to in 2.14, adds mystery and charm to her loveliness.

The motif of the dove appears in one other instance in the Song, in the voice of the turtledove which signals that spring has come and that the time for love is near (2.12). It is on hearing the voice of the turtle-dove that her lover anticipates hearing the woman's voice (2.14) in response to his own (2.8). On addressing her as a dove (2.14) he encourages her to participate in the preparations for love already evident in nature.

Nature is not idealized in the Song, however. The lions and leopards which inhabit the formidable mountain tops of Senir and Hermon, and the little foxes who ravage the orchards and vineyards of the cultivated countryside, are the counterparts in the natural world of the woman's brothers and the city watchmen, and constitute the enemies of love. The power of foxes to destroy a good crop is noted in the Samson story (Judg. 15.4-5). The danger presented by leopards and lions is also well documented in the Old Testament (Jer. 5.6; Hos. 13.7).

The precise meaning of the imperative of 2.15 has been widely discussed. It has been read as a wish spoken by either lover that nothing be allowed to harm the woman, who at that moment reaches maturity and blossoms like a fruitful vine. It may also refer to nubile, young women whom their contemporaries are eager to set upon. The little foxes would

---

20. 4.1 echoes 1.15 but for the addition of this final colon, 4.1c.

therefore correspond to the eager young men of Egyptian love songs. A third proposition, that of Delitzsch (1875), and the one preferred here, is that the imperative articulates the wish, common to both lovers, that nothing be allowed to spoil their love. The imperative follows the male lover's wooing of the woman (2.10-14) and precedes their union, to which she responds with a song of praise (2.16). The speaker of 2.15 is passed over in silence, for whoever speaks, speaks for them both. It is a word murmured in anticipation, a word not about her, nor about any other young women, but about their relationship. The pronoun 'our' which accompanies the vineyards in 2.15d, is the decisive clue.

The menace constituted by the foxes is diffused by the diminutive 'little', which precedes the noun in the second colon (2.15b). The adjective lends a teasing element to their destructiveness. The little foxes are not a real danger but only an annoying menace to the security of the vineyard. The rapid incursions they might make are suggested by the form of the verse; each of the two principal clauses (2.15ac) is taken up and developed in a second colon (2.15bd) which to a large extent repeats the material of the first. The verse thereby appears to advance in steps.

A graver threat is constituted by the lions and leopards that roam the peaks of Senir and Hermon and from which the lovers flee (4.8). Fox (1985: 134-35) points out that these animals and place-names have been deliberately chosen because of their phonetic association with the delights of the secluded garden (4.12–5.1) with which the mountain peaks form an awesome contrast. Indeed the wild beasts never approach the lovers to harm them. They rather constitute a wild and majestic backdrop to their love.

Pastoral Imagery

Certain aspects of the Song encourage comparison with the pastoral poetry of the Greek bucolic poets and particularly with that of Theocritus (284–275 BCE).[21] The presence of parallel images and of parallel forms and above all the way in which the countryside is pervaded by courtly imagery have all been noted.[22] There are however important divergences

21. See Ryken 1974: 234-35; Landy 1983: 26-32, 174; Fisch 1988: 80-81.
22. Fisch (1988: 80-81) shows that the imagery of 1.9 is comparable to that of Theocritus's eighteenth idyll (*Idyll* 18.30-31). He also compares the imagery of 2.15 to that of his fifth idyll (*Idyll* 5.113-14). Ryken (1974: 234-35) argues that the well-

which prevent the identification of the Song with the genre.

First of all, whereas for the classical poets an idealized pastoral scene provides the setting for a love song sung by a shepherd-poet, in the Song there is neither the same consistency of context nor of character. Here, pastoral images take their place among a range of different settings, each of which serves to illuminate different aspects of the love affair, and the figure of the shepherd is neither the narrator nor principal character but rather one of the guises in which the woman (1.8) or more often her lover (1.7; 2.16; 6.2) appears. In contrast too to the predominantly male perspective of the classical idyll,[23] the Song is sung principally from the woman's point of view. The immediacy of her experience, moreover, is very different from the measured third-person narration of Theocritus's idylls. Finally, the pastoral is characterized by a lighthearted playfulness absent from the Song.[24] In the Song, love is a matter of great urgency, and the longing of the lovers for each other is a consuming fire (8.6). Their love is at once secure and under threat, menaced by little foxes (2.15), lions and leopards (4.8), the counterparts in the natural world of the city watchmen (5.7) and the woman's brothers (1.6) who seek to do her harm. Moreover, whereas the death of the shepherd is a traditional subject in the classical pastoral,[25] death is set against love in the Song, as contradictory to and in opposition to life (8.6).

The pastoral imagery in the Song has also elicited the interest of proponents of the cultic theory. Kramer (1969) has drawn attention to

established forms of pastoral literature are evident in the Song. They are the invitation to love (2.10-15; 7.10-13), declarations in praise of the woman's beauty (2.1-3a; 4.1-5, 12-15; 5.12-13; 7.1-9) and descriptions of the delights of love, using rural images and metaphors (1.14, 16-17; 2.3, 16; 4.16; 5.1; 6.2-3). Ryken (1974: 221), Landy (1983: 26-27) and Fisch (1988: 80) all agree that the integration of courtly imagery into a pastoral setting is characteristic of pastoral literature.

23. In Theocritus's *Thyrsis*, a shepherd-poet sings of a shepherd lover. In *The Serenade*, a goatherd serenades his mistress, Amaryllis. In *The Goatherd and the Shepherd*, these two main characters vie with each other to sing the best song. In each, as in many of the idylls of Theocritus, the (male) shepherd-poet sings of love, either from his own personal experience or as it affects others.

24. The introduction to Theocritus's sixth idyll demonstrates the lighthearted tone of many of the idylls: 'Damoetas and Goat-herd Daphis, Aratus...had driven, each his herd together to a single spot at noon of a summer's day, and sitting them down side by side at a water-spring began to sing' (Edmonds 1912: 85, *Idyll* 6.3-4).

25. The motif is found in Theocritus's first idyll *Thyrsis*, for example, where an ideal shepherd pines and dies for love of a woman he may not court.

the Sumerian sacred marriage songs in which the shepherd-king Dumuzi
marries his sister Inanna in order to procure fertility for the land and
prosperity for its inhabitants. Pope (1977: 334-35) cites the lines of one
of these songs in which Inanna's presence is to 'bless the stall'. He
reminds us that Dumuzi too, the shepherd-king, is frequently associated
with the sheepfold and that he encourages his 'sister' to observe the
copulation of his sheep as a prelude to their own lovemaking. Pope
implies that the relevance of these passages to the pastoral images in the
Song is clear. On the contrary however it is very unclear, for nowhere is
there the suggestion in the Song that pastoral imagery has anything to
do with fertility rites. Fertility is not the issue. Rather it is love.

It is in 1.7-8 that pastoral imagery is present most clearly and
consistently. For the first and only time, the lovers are to be found in a
bucolic setting, shepherding. These verses alone, however, are not
enough to suggest that the three main characters in the Song are a
shepherd, a shepherdess and Solomon, as proponents of the dramatic
theory (Ginsburg, Renan) imply.

The woman's request is for a rendezvous, for a moment's rest and
repose with her lover in the middle of the day, for even as she enjoys his
presence, either actual or imagined, she is aware that the solitary duties
of shepherding to which they must both attend will, for a time, separate
them. Her question, which is simple and direct, is therefore full of
longing; it is all the more so given the duplication of the interrogative
'êkâ, 'where', and the multiplicity of long open vowels which characterize the first and second colons (1.7). There is also the lengthy form of
address, 'you whom my soul loves', which is unique to the Song. It
adds to longing a hint of melancholy; not only does she want to find out
where he is, but perhaps even more urgently, she wants to communicate
to him how much she misses him. She has barely given him the time to
reply when, in 1.7, longing gives way to angry frustration. She suddenly
accuses him of indifference or even callousness towards her, depending
on the force of the participle 'ot^{e}yâ, to be examined in due course.

His response is equally direct (cf. Landy 1983: 169-76). He issues
specific instructions yet his meaning is far from clear. It all depends on
whether it is his sheep she is directed to follow and whether she is
capable of discerning the tracks of his sheep from those of the others.
More importantly, it depends on his tone of voice and the intention of
his words whether his instructions constitute a straightforward assurance
of his love for her (if he is where he commands her to go) or the teasing

rebuff she most fears (if he sends her in search of him in vain). She will either be greeted by her loved one who awaits her or she will be shamed by him and made to look like a vagabond or even a prostitute if he does not appear. Indeed the possibilities are yet more numerous, for if he is where he directs her to go, namely by the shepherds' tents, there is no guarantee that his friends will not be there also. The decision as to whether he will acknowledge her before his friends is also undisclosed. The woman may equally be received or rejected by her lover. Love makes her vulnerable, ready for commitment but open also to betrayal.

Some critics question the identity of the speaker in 1.8. Landy (1983: 170) and Fox (1985: 103) agree that the speaker is the man. Gordis (1974: 80) suggests that it is his companions that reply. If so, then the woman has cause for anxiety, for the response of his male companions underlines her lover's absence.

None of these questions can be answered, yet perhaps they do not matter too much. The meaning of the dialogue is to be found not so much in the words themselves as in the speech of the lovers who woo each other by the sheer sound of each other's voice. Thus, as Landy (1983: 175) points out, whereas the dialogue at one level reveals anger, fear and evasiveness, at the level of structure and sound it discloses a most profound unity.

The verses also are perfectly balanced. The woman's question in 1.7a is countered by the man's response in 1.8a. Both are expressed as impersonal constructions. The lengthy term of address 'you whom my soul loves' (1.7b) is balanced by an equally lengthy term of address, 'fairest among women' (1.8b) in the same position in the next verse. Her twin questions (1.7c-d) each begun by the question 'where?' find an answer in the two imperatives he issues in 1.8c-d. In both verses, the final colon seals the enigma (1.7e, 8e).

In addition to the harmonious form of these verses is the alliterative unity created by sounds which echo each other throughout. We have already noted the assonance in 1.7ab and the effect of long open vowels in the creation of an atmosphere of longing. We should also note the alliteration of *y, r, s* in *tarbîs bassohorayîm* (1.7c) and the way in which the sound of these letters helps to evoke the sun's fierce heat. His words too are characterized by alliteration and assonance; in particular we should note the kinship of *sᵉ'î/hasso'n* (1.8b) and *ûrᵉ'î/haroʿîm* (1.8de).

The effect of the density of similar sounds, in a perfectly balanced construction, is to wean us away from a search for meaning which is independent from sensory experience and sound. The lovers speak to each other in a language that only lovers understand, in riddles, in communication which has become play. Through sound and form they have found a way of giving voice to their love. It is, in some sense, a speaking in tongues.

The pastoral milieu, now that it has established itself, does not surprise us when it reappears. It does so in two very similar passages, 4.1-2 and 6.5-6. In neither is the pastoral imagery ostensibly the object of interest. In both cases the imagery is descriptive of the woman's beauty although it is developed to such a degree as to take on a life of its own.

In both passages her hair is likened to a flock of goats moving down the slopes of Gilead (4.1; 6.5). The image is full of movement. Anyone who has watched goats on a hillside will recall their sure-footedness and their speed. The image therefore successfully describes her head of tumultuous curls. The descent of the goats is balanced by the ascent of the ewes and their young from the water (4.2; 6.6), an image from the same milieu, chosen to express the whiteness and perfect formation of her teeth.

The movement of the flocks up and down the hillside creates a pleasing harmony appropriate to the descriptive song. It also helps to anchor the lovers in the external world which is imbued with their presence. The fact that this imagery appears twice, almost without distinction, creates the impression of the semi-permanence of the pastoral background. This is only an impression, however, for all the imagery in the Song is shifting and temporary, forever subordinate to the primacy of the lovers and their love.

There is one last aspect of the pastoral theme to consider. The poet takes advantage of the fact that the verb *r'h*, to feed, can be used both transitively, in the sense of pasturing one's flock, and intransitively, meaning to eat. This flexibility lends a certain suggestiveness to his language; the male protagonist is both a shepherd who grazes his flock and an eager lover who feeds on his beloved. Once the language of eating and drinking has established itself as an image of lovemaking, the intransitive sense of the verb *r'h* presses ever more closely to the surface. It is sometimes even present when the verb is used primarily in a transitive sense.

The verb first appears in 1.7 in the woman's question to her lover, 'Where do you graze?' The object 'flock' is understood. The Hebrew however is deliberately terse. It leaves it up to the hearer to constitute the scene. Indeed one might envisage it differently on a second reading of the Song.

Of greater ambiguity is the statement in 2.16, 'he grazes among the water-lilies'. All depending on whether the participle *haro'eh* is used here transitively or intransitively and whether the flowers indicate what is eaten or the place of feeding, the phrase could mean that the lover feeds on the flowers, that he feeds on something else among the flowers or that he pastures his flock among the flowers.

Each of these options describe his delight in a slightly different way. In the first, the flowers on which he feeds are a metaphor for the woman. By implication, the young lover appears in the guise of an animal who feeds on them. According to the second reading, it is she whom her lover finds among the water-lilies as he grazes his flock there. The third possibility is that the phrase is a straightforward metaphor for the delight he takes in her; he rejoices in her as a flock among tender water-lilies. The fourth and final possibility is that the phrase does not refer to the woman specifically at all. It is simply an evocation of bucolic delight in accordance with the general atmosphere.

Only the last interpretation, which is also the most literal, would seem to be unlikely. Indeed the reason why we look for other, metaphorical readings is because the intention of the phrase is clearly to explain the preceding sentence (2.16). In other words it is to specify in what way the lovers belong to each other.

The phrase may refer specifically to their kisses, for her lips are compared to water-lilies in 5.13. Alternatively the reference is to lovemaking more generally, the water-lilies being one of the flowers of her garden which she invites him to come and eat (4.16). The image is at any rate one of great delicacy and refinement. The lover pastures not on rough pastureland but on tender flowers. Though a shepherd, he has never ceased to be a king.

The mirror of this passage is 6.2-3. Here the declaration of mutual belonging (6.3) interrupts a series of images in which the language of pasturing joins the image of the garden to express the lovers' joy. It is indeed fitting that the image of the garden and pastoral imagery should find each other, for the water-lilies on which he feeds and which also describe his lips (5.13) grow nowhere better than in a carefully tended garden.

One further such image remains, that of 4.5 in which her breasts are compared to fawns, twins of a gazelle, feeding among the water-lilies.

This image was discussed above. Suffice therefore to say that it is an image of great delicacy and one which is evocative of restful repose. This is especially so since gazelles are elsewhere associated with swiftness of movement (2.17; 8.14). Here at last they are at peace feeding on water-lilies. Her lover is similarly at peace at her breast. He feeds on her with infinite delight.

Three homophonic roots are fused in the verb *r'h*, the most common of which is the verb 'to feed' or 'to graze'. It is this root which has been considered at length. In addition however is the Aramaic verb *r''* which has given the Hebrew *re'a*, meaning 'desire' or 'will'. There is also the Hebrew verb *r'h*, 'to associate with'. It gives the noun *re'*, a 'companion' or 'attendant' and *ra'yâ*, a female version of the same. The latter appears in the Song as the term of address most frequently used by the man of the woman (1.9, 15; 2.1, 10, 13). She however uses the masculine form only once (*re'î*, 5.16). Much more often she uses *dôdî* with which *re'î* occurs in parallelism in 5.16. Indeed, that the feminine form of the noun is used so frequently in the Song is in itself unusual, for nowhere else does it appear in the Old Testament except perhaps in Judg. 11.37 in the *kethib* reading. The masculine plural *re'* (*re'îm*) appears in 5.1 of the lover's companions. They are invited to eat and drink their fill.

Given the limited, yet constant presence of pastoral imagery, the poet could hardly have failed to intend a play on words. The young man is a shepherd (*ro'eh*) grazing (*haro'eh*) among the water-lilies which are a metaphor for his lover (*ra'yâ*). Together, they find sustenance, but most importantly delight.

Vines and Vineyards

The blossoming vines are numbered among the many signs of Spring (2.13; 7.12).[26] They are part of the new growth in which the lovers see the flourishing and burgeoning of their love (2.13; 7.12). There is the hint however that the vineyard sometimes takes on a symbolic dimension, as representative of the woman or of her relationship with her lover. In contrast to the garden, which is a place of unsullied delight for the lovers, a place where they are withdrawn from the world and free of its

---

26. Spring is not mentioned as such. Instead it is evoked by the passing of the winter and the accompanying rain (2.11). *s͏ᵉtaw* is unique to the Song and, according to Wagner (1966: 79), is an Aramaism. The Arabic cognate *sita* designates both rain and winter.

cares, the vineyard is presented primarily as a valuable asset, liable to despoliation and in need of constant care and attention. In contrast to the garden which is presented as a place of paradisaical pleasure, the presentation of the vineyard is much more concerned with the socio-economic realities of owning and maintaining it.

The first hint that the vineyard might refer to something other than external reality comes towards the end of 1.6. In the course of the verse, the vineyards entrusted to the woman's care (1.6d) are contrasted with her own vineyard which has fallen into disrepair (1.6e). The exclamation 'My own vineyard I did not tend' may indeed refer to an actual vineyard. It may indeed be the exasperated cry of an overworked woman on whom her brothers have placed an impossible burden for some reason. It may also be another way of saying that she has spent herself working for siblings who fail to care about her. The anger of her brothers and the relationship of this anger to her present situation is also unexplained. Her servitude in their vineyard may on the one hand be the cause of her self-neglect. Alternatively it may be their way of punishing her for the violation of some unspecified norm. Whatever lies behind the neglected vineyard, it is a perfect image of the shame and rejection she feels.

As already argued in the section on *Regal Imagery*, 8.11-12 forms an *inclusio* with 1.5-6 in the light of which the riddle of 8.11-12 cedes a little of its enigma. It does so in so far as the reference to 'my own vineyard' is most likely to be understood figuratively, for this same expression is used in 1.6e as a metaphor for the woman. We have also established that it is most likely the woman who is the speaker, an interpretation which accords well with the triumphant tone of the previous verse (8.10) and with the convention that the initiative of the lover is usually limited to the description of her (1.9-11; 4.1-15; 6.4-10; 7.2-7) or dialogue with her (1.15-17; 2.1-2; 2.10-15; 4.16–5.1). We recall that in the course of the parable, every effort is made to emphasize the high value of Solomon's vineyard in order to contrast it with a particular vineyard, 'my own vineyard', which is beyond compare (8.12). The woman wants nothing of Solomon or of his money, nothing of the exploitative relationships which made her the servant of her brothers. Love has given her her independence. With this new-found freedom she makes the gift of herself.

2.10-15 closes in with an urgent imperative to protect the vineyards from the foxes which would ravage the vines. Its position at the end of the man's invitation encourages the reader to suppose that the image of the vineyard refers not only to the blossoming vines around them (cf. 2.13), but to their relationship which is under threat even as they come close to consummating it. The shift from vineyards in general in 2.15c to 'our vineyards' in 2.15d is enough to suggest that the reference is to the lovers who are full of longing for each other. The declaration of mutual love in 2.16 strengthens this interpretation.

In each of these passages, 1.6, 2.15-16 and 8.11-12, the image of the vineyard must be handled with great care, for the secondary, figurative meanings of which there is only a hint are difficult to grasp. They lie just beneath the surface and participate in the general atmosphere of love and longing which pervades the countryside.

The image of wine is related to that of vines and vineyards; just as the blossoming vines anticipate the lovers' meeting (2.13; 6.11; 7.12), so the finest wine describes their long-awaited embrace (1.2; 4.10). On her lips, the image expresses intense longing (1.2). On his, it is an exclamation of sheer joy (4.10). In each instance the comparison is followed by a reference to the fragrance of the loved one's oils (1.3a; 4.10c). The reference to the scent of the vines in 2.13 brings together and projects into the natural world certain aspects of both these images; whereas in 1.2-3 and 4.10 the image of wine relates to the taste of the loved one's kisses, in 2.13 the scent of the vines is a sign of spring. To the lovers, however, they convey much more than that; their burgeoning anticipates reunion with the loved one who is tasted, touched and felt.

A third verse, 7.10, bears some similarity to 1.2 and 4.10, for here the woman's kisses, literally 'her palate', are compared to the 'finest wine'. The full impact of the dialogue is discerned in the wider context of the verse, for the comparison of her kisses to 'finest wine' is the cumulation of a description which began in 7.8 in praise of her stature, a description which takes on a life of its own as the eager lover determines to climb the palm tree and grasp its fronds.[27] The desire to 'grasp' his loved one, acknowledged in 7.9b, is subsequently linked specifically to her breasts (7.9c) which are compared to the clusters of the vine (7.9d). Then, as in 1.2 and 4.10, touching his lover also makes him aware of her fragrance. Thus it is that he wishes aloud (7.9c-e):

---

27. *sansinnâw*, its fronds, is a *hapax legomenon* but is related to the Akkadian *sissinu*, 'the upper branches of a date palm' (Fox 1985: 163).

Oh may your breasts be like clusters of the vine,
and your breath sweet-scented like apples.

In 7.10 this wish is unexpectedly fulfilled, for no sooner has he filled
out his longing with another expression of desire for her kisses (7.10c),
than she responds by completing the sentence on his behalf (7.10b). The
comparison of her kisses to wine, which flows from one lover to the
other, corresponds to the culmination of the sequence.

Some of the main differences between the image of the vineyard
and that of the garden have been noted. There are, however, certain
similarities. Both are marked off for a particular purpose, the vineyard
for cultivation, the garden for pleasure. Both, at times, symbolize the
unique integrity of the woman. The two images are brought yet closer
together by means of the network of motifs which they share; wine is
discovered in the garden of the woman (5.1), just as wine, in 1.2 and
4.10, is associated with the exchange of kisses. Characteristic of these
kisses is the joyful recognition of the fragrance of each other's oils, a
fragrance which is present both in the blossoming vines (2.13) and in the
garden (4.16). Moreover the fragrance of the garden is that of the spices
that grow therein (4.14; 5.1), the same spices to which her oils are
compared in 4.10.

Many of these associations come together in the woman's promise to
give her lover 'spiced wine' to drink (8.2c). The reference to wine is
reminiscent of the association between drink and lovemaking (1.2;
4.10),[28] just as the spices which give it a special tang are reminiscent of
the delights of her garden (4.14; 5.1). The mention of pomegranates
(8.2d) consolidates this association, for they too grow in abundance
there. The pronominal suffix *î* in 1.6, 2.15 and 8.12, is a clue to the
symbolic dimensions of the imagery. The offer of 'the juice of my
pomegranates' is none other than the offer of her breasts.

One final reference to wine remains, that of 7.3, in which the
woman's navel is likened to a rounded bowl. So lovely is the bowl that
it is the wish of her lover that it never may lack wine,[29] the exact word

---

28. We should note here the technique called paronomasia by means of which her
yearning to kiss her lover (*'eššaqᵉka*, 8.1) is associated with drinking (*'ašqᵉka*, 8.2).
The association is already familiar to the reader (cf. 1.2; 5.1; 7.10). The originality of
8.1-2 is in the harmony of sound between tenor and vehicle.

29. *'al-yeḥsar* is to be understood as an emphatic negation rather than as a
prohibition (Joüon 1947: 311, fig. 114k).

for which is a *hapax* in the Old Testament.[30] Wine here is not an image of lovemaking but rather of abundance and plenitude. It is set alongside a similar image, that of a pile of wheat (7.3). Spring, with its blossoming vines, is no longer the implied season. Rather it is autumn.

The Garden

Gardens enjoyed a long tradition in the ancient Near East. The Egyptians, whose economic life was centred around the Nile, were the first to develop the formal, geometrical garden built around a complex system of canals and storage pools. These provided the water essential for the irrigation of vines and fruit trees. To this basic arrangement were added figs and palms for shade, and flowers for decoration. In contrast to the enclosed Egyptian garden is the royal park. This large, wooded hunting preserve was the innovation of the Assyrian kings. Like the Egyptians, the Assyrians built, in these areas, small temples for cultic use and outdoor pavilions for royal feasts. With the expansion of the Persian Empire and the conquest of Egypt in 525 BCE, the Persians conceived of a garden which combined these two traditions, that of the enclosed garden and the royal park. The result was a *pairidaeza*, the Hebrew form of which, *pardes*, appears in the Song at 4.13, in Eccl. 2.5 and Neh. 2.9.

Given that such a well-established tradition of garden-making existed in the ancient Near East, and in view of the influence of the Egyptians, Assyrians and Persians successively in Palestine, it is not surprising that there is evidence in the Old Testament of an indigenous Hebrew garden tradition. We read of royal gardens (Est. 1.5; 7.7; 2 Kgs 25.4; Neh. 3.15; Jer. 39.4; 52.7), of garden pavilions therein (Est. 1.5; 7.7) and of garden tombs in which the patrons buried their dead (2 Kgs 21.18, 26). Isaiah also hints that certain Israelites participated in cultic practices carried out there (Isa. 66.17).

Pope (1977: 210-29) has explored extensively the relationship between Canaanite mortuary rites, the garden and the language of love. He suggests that the Song belongs to a love feast in a garden tomb, executed ritually, in defiance of death. Such an interpretation, however, depends solely on a secondary function of the garden, namely that of

---

30. *mezeg* is probably an Aramaism (Wagner 1966: 73-74) related to the Hebrew *mesek* found only in Ps. 75.9. The verb *msk* is rather more common (Isa. 19.14; Ps. 102.10).

providing a place of burial. It forgets that the garden was primarily a place of pleasure and of relaxation.

The spices and trees which grow in the garden of the Song (4.12–5.1) evoke the splendour of the ancient Assyrian royal gardens. Tiglath Pileser I, Sennacherib and Cyrus all took great pride in planting in their gardens exotic species gained in their forays abroad. Moreover, the booth or wine house, to which the man takes the woman in 2.4, reminds us of the marquee in Queen Esther's garden or more distantly of King Assurbanipal's banquet out of doors. For both of these reasons the motif is clearly not a funerary but a courtly one. At the very least, it belongs to a milieu of opulence such as that described in Eccl. 2.5. It is also an important bridge between the courtly and natural world, for in the garden, nature is harnessed, civilized.

Gardens—like islands—exercise upon the imagination a marvellous fascination. It is all the more potent an image in the ancient Near East where, over against the dryness of the desert, the garden, watered by streams and teeming with vegetation, is a symbol of life and hope. Indeed the garden is a symbol of paradise for the three great religions of the Middle East, Judaism, Christianity and Islam. The origins of this symbolism are, moreover, extremely ancient.

Characteristics of the garden are evident in the eulogy of Dilmun, in the Myth of Enki and Ninhursag. Dilmun is a divine paradise to which humanity has no access, that is, except for Ziusudra, the Sumerian Noah, who was exceptionally admitted there by Enlil (*ANET*: 44, ll. 252-61). Even though it is reserved for the gods alone, it nevertheless expresses the deepest aspirations of humankind, for it is a place of external youth from which sickness, conflict and death are excluded (*ANET*: 38, ll. 1-30). Although it is not described as a garden explicitly, but rather as a 'land' (*ANET*: 38, l. 1) or as a 'city' (*ANET*: 38, l. 30), characteristics of the garden do pertain, in the water which enables farms and fields to appear (*ANET*: 39, ll. 31-64), in the presence of a 'gardener' who bears cucumbers, apples and grapes to the god Enki (*ANET*: 39-40, ll. 153-67) and in the proliferation of plants following the impregnation of Ninhursag by Enki (*ANET*: 40, ee. 86-95).

Another Sumerian text speaks of a divine paradise at Eridu,[31] at the mouth of two rivers. In its midst grows a mysterious tree, its roots sunk deep in the fertilizing waters. Again the image of the garden is not explicitly mentioned. It may be argued however that a garden is the

31. See Widengren (1951: 5-6) on *CT* XVI Pl. 46.183–47.198.

earthly model for the divine paradise, since only an oasis or a garden with its irrigation canals and pools could sustain such life as this. Indeed oases are themselves organized by irrigation systems which make them metaphorical 'gardens'. Jericho is an extremely ancient example. Moreover the title of 'gardener' was given to King Sargon at his birth (*ANET*: 119, l. 11). He was appointed as the 'gardener' of the god Akki. The mythological background of the text is hinted at by the appearance of the goddess Ishtar who falls in love with the gardener-king (*ANET*: 119, e.12). In the Gilgamesh Epic her love for Išullanu is alluded to (*ANET*: 84, l. 64). He too is described as a 'gardener'.

The image of the garden therefore has a long history in the mythical imagination of Semitic peoples. From the beginning it is associated with the paradisiacal realm of the gods. Closely related to the theme of the paradisiacal garden is the 'land of the living' of the Sumerian Gilgamesh Epic (*ANET*: 48-50). It is a land far off and inaccessible, zealously guarded by the monster Huwawa. Gilgamesh, in search of immortality, sets out to fell its cedars, the symbolic counterpart of the plant of life wrested from him in the Akkadian story (*ANET*: 96, ll. 288-89). The enterprise however fails, for although Gilgamesh and his companion penetrate the forest and slay the monster, still the god Enlil denies him external life (*ANET*: 50, ll. 32-34).

In the Old Testament the ancient idea of a paradisiacal garden of the gods has not been lost. Two passages in particular, Ezekiel 28 and 31, recall the ancient motif. In Ezekiel 28 the 'garden of the lord', the garden of Eden, is situated on 'God's holy mountain' (Ezek. 28.14).[32] It was inhabited by the pharaoh of Egypt who was expelled on account of his over-weening pride (Ezek. 28.17). In Ezekiel 31, 'the garden of God' (Ezek. 31.8, 9, 16) is associated not only with Eden (Ezek. 31.9) but also with Lebanon (Ezek. 31.16) and with a prodigiously tall cedar (Ezek. 31.3) which was destroyed also on account of its pride (Ezek. 31.10-11).

As Gibson (1981: 106) suggests, the allusion is probably to an ancient story about the home of the gods and about how, once upon a time, a rebellious angel was expelled for challenging the father of the gods, El. In both passages the rebellious angel has been historicized so as to be identified with the pharaoh of Egypt (Ezek. 31.19) or the king of Tyre (Ezek. 28.9). Stolz (1972: 141-56) goes further. He relates the motif of

---

32. As Wyatt (1986: 426) has pointed out, the mountain, like the garden, functions as an omphalos motif. These are not different locations but different accounts of the same theme.

the cedar tree to the Gilgamesh Epic, to the search for immortality and the motif of the tree of life.

The garden of Eden, described by the priestly writer in Genesis 2–3, is no longer a garden of the gods but a garden created by God for humankind. The mythological inheritance of the story is everywhere evident—in the presence of the tree of life (Gen. 2.9) and in the serpent (Gen. 3.1, 4, 13, 14), both of which recall the Gilgamesh story—yet it is no longer a tragic story about the human search for immortality and its failure. It is rather a story about human disobedience before a divine command and the loss of innocence which results. Rather than being about life and death, it is about knowledge and responsibility; it tells how human beings, by overstepping the limits of their existence, brought upon themselves all the cares which accompany the power and independence of God. Henceforth, we are all beyond the garden, longing for our return. The image is used by the prophets of the return of the exiles (Isa. 51.3; 58.11; Jer. 31.12). It is no less potent a symbol for us, evocative of all our nostalgia for perfect peace.

The garden of the Song and the garden of Eden have often been compared, even though they are different in genre—the one is narrative, the other poetry[33]—for the two texts function as a diptych in the exploration of human relationships. The story in Genesis explores the disparity between humanity's potential and its actual state, locating the responsibility for such a situation in an act of disobedience which ruptured humanity's harmonious relationship with its Creator and the world around it. It is a story which seeks to explain why human life is riven with pain and suffering and why human relationships are often more conflictual than we would desire them to be. If the garden of Eden story is about dislocation and exile, and if it asks questions for which there are no easy answers, the Song on the other hand simply sings of love, and in so doing, initiates a process of restoration and return. It is not that the world is repaired and that suffering ceases to exist—the element of menace is too powerfully present in the Song for that—but simply that love transforms all things. Barriers, in the eyes of love, are thresholds, and divisions, distinctions. The garden, which in the Genesis story becomes an inaccessible place from which humanity is exiled, in the Song is rediscovered in the woman; it is in union or communion with her that her lover rediscovers the bliss of which the Eden story spoke.

33. Comparative studies have already been undertaken by Trible (1978: 144-65) and Landy (1983: 183-268).

As a result, the world around is also recreated; it too becomes a garden, a garden of love which the reader too may enter for a time.

The garden of the Song is however, like the garden of Eden, infinitely discreet. It appears first, in 4.12a, as an image of the woman. She is, however, simultaneously described as a sealed spring (4.12b). The question is, therefore, whether she is the garden or the life within it. The suggestion is that she is both. The same ambivalence is present in the location of the garden. At first, the readers suppose that it grows around the spring (4.12). Then, in 4.15, we wonder if the spring rises elsewhere. Perhaps in Lebanon? Moreover the garden and the spring have, by this stage, altered considerably; no longer is it a question of a single enclosed garden, but of a multiplicity of gardens growing around a well of rushing waters (4.15).[34] The relationship between Lebanon and the garden is a further source of ambiguity. The woman, who is summoned from the heights in 4.8, and in whose clothes its scent lingers in 4.11, is identified with Lebanon in 4.15. The garden, which would seem to be the opposite of Lebanon in terms of safety and seclusion, is paradoxically brought into some undefined relationship with it.

The result of the unsteadiness of the poet's gaze is to convey something of the lively mystery of her person; she is like a sealed spring (4.12b), she is chaste, yet she is also like a well of living water (4.15a) whose influence spreads far beyond her. This liveliness can also be described in terms of the freedom of the mountain streams rushing down the slopes of Lebanon (4.15b), or in terms of the abundance of an exotic garden, filled with every kind of tree and fruit (4.13-14). The woman is, to her lover, each and all of these things; it is this extraordinary ensemble which bewilders and enchants him. Yet more significant is the erotic dimension lent to this sequence by the organizing image of the garden. It describes, with great delicacy, how she progressively opens herself to her lover and invites him to delight in her. It is to this movement that we now turn.

After having addressed her in the second person in order to ask her to leave Lebanon and its attendant dangers (4.9), he continues to speak directly to her, describing the sweetness of her kisses and the sensuous scent of her garments (4.11). As their intimacy grows, however, and

---

34. As argued in the section on *Water*, Murphy (1990: 157) suggests that the expression *ma'yan gannîm* may be a plural of generalization. To render by the singular 'a garden fountain' does however lessen the effect of proliferation which the passage in various ways emphasizes.

likewise his respect for her, he begins to speak to her in the third person and to address her in this rather more detached manner (4.12-13). He does so in order to emphasize her independence and, in particular, her virginity. Neither is to be wrested from her, yet his very reticence, conveyed by the seemingly decisive passive participles 'locked' and 'sealed', heightens the tension in which he waits. They barely conceal his impatience for the garden to open and the fountain to flow.

Contributive also to this tension is the echo of the first image *gan na'ûl* in the second colon (4.12b) and its close relationship to the second element in the pair *ma'yan ḥatûm*, by means of assonance. A further tension, subordinated by the LXX, is the shift in the MT from *gan* to *gal* in 4.12b. This option disturbs neither the meaning nor the sound of the line; both *beth* and *lamedh* are already alliterative and a garden or pool are equally appropriate in the context. It is a question simply of emphasis. Equally ambiguous is the meaning of *š^elaḥayik* in 4.13; the reference is either to vegetation, to the shoots of plants growing in the garden, or to the canals which water them.[35] The ambiguity of the term strengthens the parallelism between spring and garden and denies the complete identification of the woman with either of them. A locked garden, or a fountain sealed, the image hints that she can barely contain the abundant life within her.

This life is presently bodied forth in an orchard of pomegranates and all choice fruits, in a garden of exotic trees and spices, which speak of her splendour, her strength, her beauty, her sweetness (4.13-15). Many of the components of this garden are already deeply embedded in the language of the Song. The tree (4.14) is a metaphor for her chivalrous lover (2.3a) and its fruit an image of his gift of himself to her (2.3c). The pomegranate (4.13) describes her rosy cheeks visible through her veil (4.3). Myrrh and frankincense (4.14) are associated with the royal procession through the wilderness (3.6), and henna and nard (4.13) with the intimacy of their embrace (1.12-14). Spices (4.14) characterize the mountains to which her lover departs at the close of the Song (8.14). They are also associated with the fragrance of the woman (4.10) and with her kisses (8.2). To these familiar elements yet more are added— calamus, cinnamon, aloes and saffron (4.14). They add scent, taste and colour to an already luxuriant garden. In it, the beauty of the natural world is tended, ordered and civilized.

35. According to this interpretation, the reference is to the *šelaḥ* of mishnaic Hebrew (*m. M. Qaṭ.* 1.1; *m. B. Bat.* 4.7: see Haupt 1902b: 203, 207).

In the course of the description of the garden, the emphasis changes from an evocation of the woman's virginal purity to the promise of life which she holds forth. Her lover continues to address her in the third person (4.15), yet it is clear that the distance between them is increasingly difficult to maintain; as soon as the closed garden (4.12c) and sealed fountain (4.12c) are brought into relationship with each other, the result is a fountain of gardens (4.15a), a well of living waters (4.15b), that is to say, multiplicity, proliferation, all the vibrancy of new life. The woman is no longer identifiable with a particular place, garden or spring. Rather, her life-giving presence gives birth to, and sustains, a multiplicity of gardens (4.15a) nourished by a water supply, arising from without and from within. Not only is the woman the garden and the source within it, but she is also the life of the world beyond and the vigour of streams arising in Lebanon (4.15b).

Up until this point (4.15), the woman herself has been silent; she has been the passive subject of her lover's praise. Even as she stirs, however, she, by now almost a universal figure, calls upon the winds of the earth likewise to 'awake' (4.16). This she does in order that the fragrance of the garden might 'stream forth', and in particular, reach her beloved whom she subsequently invites to come and eat (4.16).[36] The initiative she takes in issuing this command constitutes the beginning of the opening of the garden; it is an invitation which is decisive yet delicate and discreet. It is also reminiscent, by contrast, of the garden of Eden story; the winds which converge upon the woman, inviting her lover to return to the garden, contrast with the four rivers that flow from Eden, disseminating its life in the world around (Gen. 2.10-14). The waters of the Song similarly converge upon the woman; she is the primordial spring in the garden (4.12) but she is also associated with the streams flowing into the garden from Lebanon (4.15).

The garden, henceforth, becomes the place of freedom and of exchange. No longer is it an image of the woman's carefully preserved independence, but of the gift of herself to her lover, for no sooner has she claimed the garden as her own (*gannî*, 4.16) than it is also his (*gannô*, 4.16).

He responds to her invitation with decisiveness and evident desire. The series of active verbs which follow, each in the first person singular (5.1), betray his eagerness to take possession of his garden and to lose himself in its plenitude. Indeed this impression is all the more forceful,

---

36. The verb used by the woman is *nzl*, the same verb used by the man in 4.15.

given the lack of verbs in the preceding passage, and the pent-up energy implied by the two passive participles 'locked' and 'sealed' (4.12) which have already been discussed. For all his haste, however, he is nevertheless a child in her arms (cf. 1.13): he comes to her as to the source in Eden, as to the first garden where innocence, love and safety are joyfully restored.

This brings us to one of the contrasts between the Song and the Genesis story: whereas, in the latter, woman is a secondary figure and the initiator of Adam's fall, in the Song, she represents the original garden and is the agent of his provisory return.[37] It is therefore significant that the image of the garden, developed over a number of verses (4.12–5.1), falls at the midpoint of the Song. The position of the image not only emphasizes the predominance of the woman, who throughout the Song plays the major part, but also echoes structurally the relationship of the woman to the world beyond, in the eyes of her loved one; the natural world and the abundance of life visible there is recreated in her, for she, to him, is the personification of its beauty.

The image of the garden reappears briefly in 6.2-3, following the experience of loss and tragedy on the part of the woman. If she has been likened to a garden, and if she has given herself as one might open a secret garden to a specially trusted friend, she is no less vulnerable to rejection and betrayal. It is particularly ironic therefore that the garden, which is an image of the profound communion of the lovers in 4.12–5.1, momentarily in 6.2 threatens to exclude the woman from the care and attention of her lover; when the daughters of Jerusalem ask her where he has gone, she replies that he has gone to his garden, the implication being that he has made himself inaccessible to her. The garden is no longer therefore a place of relationship but of solitude:

> My beloved has gone down to his garden
> to the beds of spices
> to graze in the gardens
> and to pick water-lilies.

The tension is eased immediately, however, with the joyful affirmation on the part of the woman that 'I am my beloved's and my beloved is

---

37. The intention of this remark is not to suggest the literary dependence of one text upon the other and so enter the question of dating. More important than the question of literary dependence is the way in which both authors use a common cultural motif, that of the garden, to different ends.

mine' (6.3), a declaration which reassures the reader that the garden of
6.2 is none other than the garden of his beloved which he has entered,
and in which he discovers his delight. The exclusion is therefore not so
much that of the woman as that of the daughters of Jerusalem, to whom
she replies from the intimacy of the garden (6.2). If they now seek to
help her (6.1), it is too late. She has found her lover and, invisible and
inaccessible to all around, she rejoices in being alone with him.

Even as the garden is, at least temporarily, a place in the external
world to which he may go (6.2), so it is also a place of reverie for him.
In 6.11 he goes down to the nut garden[38] in the hope of seeing signs of
spring. Although, unlike Eden, the garden is part of the world of season
and change, it is nevertheless like Eden a place apart, the garden of his
heart which reveals to him the miraculous presence of love (6.2). The
confusion at the level of language (see p. 30, n. 16) speaks evocatively of
his surprise.

In the closing verses, the association of the garden with the woman
continues, though not in the same way as in 4.12–5.1. In 8.13 she is seen
sitting in the gardens with a captive audience around her. The use of the
image of the garden is, by this stage, highly complex. It refers primarily
to the setting in which the woman and the young women find themselves, a garden-complex. On the basis of the private symbolism which
grows between the lovers and which identifies the garden with the
woman, it is tempting to understand the many gardens of the garden-
complex as an allusion to her young friends. They come to her for
wisdom and advice, for she has come to inhabit the place which symbolically represents her. Meanwhile, her companion is distanced from her
spatially, and is freed to roam the mountains of spices which are his
particular domain (cf. 2.17). She, the heroine of the Song, has the last
word; not only does she dismiss her lover, but she instructs others,
presumably in the art of love.

Water

While the recurrence of certain images establishes the continuity of their
experience, the increasing prominence of water imagery echoes the
growth of love. It is this movement that will be considered now.

In 1.7 there is no explicit reference to water at all. The woman simply

---

38. *'egôz* is a *hapax legomenon* in the Old Testament though in postbiblical
Hebrew it is used of nuts in general and of walnuts in particular.

asks where her lover grazes, where he lies down at noon, presumably to water and graze his flock. Water is present only implicitly in the imagined scene. Nor is there any explicit reference to water in 1.14 save in the place-name Ein-Gedi, literally the 'spring' or 'eye of a kid', the well-known oasis by the Dead Sea. The association of a kid with water is perhaps meant to make us cast our minds back briefly to the response made to the woman in 1.8, where she is to follow the tracks of the flock and pasture her kids by the shepherds' tents. The place-name Ein-Gedi strengthens retrospectively the image of the thirsty flock seeking water at noon. Finally, there is no direct reference to water in 4.2. Its presence is strongly implied, however, by the reference to 'the washing' from which the shorn ewes emerge, sparkling white (4.2, cf. 6.6).

The first explicit reference to water comes unexpectedly in 4.12 in association with the image of the garden. Even here, however, the imagery is only potential, for the woman is described as a spring that is sealed,[39] even as she is also a garden that is locked:

> A garden locked is my sister, my bride,
> a garden locked, a fountain sealed.

Even as the spring cannot be contained, but wells up and overflows, so the garden does finally open, first of all almost imperceptibly in the *šᵉlaḥayim* of 4.13a. As already noted, it is uncertain to which sphere of influence they belong, garden or spring, for the form may refer to the irrigation canals which the sealed spring covertly feeds and which immediately bring forth an orchard of pomegranates. Alternatively it may refer to vegetation, to the shoots of new growth that the mere presence of a spring provokes. The most important aspect of the form, however, is the verb from which it comes, namely *šlḥ*, 'to send', on account of its energy and dynamism. The immediate consequence of this 'sending forth' is the appearance of exotic trees and spices which fill her lover with delight (4.13, 14):

---

39. It is noteworthy that the image of the sealed spring is also used by the author of Proverbs with reference to female sexuality. It appears in the context of a reproof to the husband who has betrayed his wife's chastity by unfaithfulness to her (Prov. 5.16). The woman of the Song could not be accused of unchastity. Indeed as Elliott (1989: 252) argues, 'The significance of these enclosed images is an absolute unavailability to anyone except the Lover. The door, the seal, the battlements do not represent her will against his desire so much as fidelity that opens and surrenders to him alone.'

> Your shoots are an orchard of pomegranates
> full of choice fruits,
> aromatic cane and cinnamon,
> every kind of frankincense tree,
> myrrh and aloes,
> indeed every exquisite spice.

Following the description of the luxuriant garden, garden and spring are brought into direct relationship with one another, for the woman is hailed as a 'garden fountain', literally 'a fountain of gardens', a fountain or spring whose waters make fertile not one, but many gardens (*gannîm*). Henceforth it is water imagery that comes to the fore and the image of the garden extensively developed in 4.13c-14 cedes to the open spaces of Lebanon (4.15b):

> A garden fountain,
> a spring of living water,
> streams flowing down from Lebanon.

The spring which gives rise to a multiplicity of gardens, the well of living waters and the streams which rush down the Lebanese hillside are all characterized by life, movement and unbounded freedom. The plural forms which characterize *gannîm*, 'gardens', *ḥayyîm*, 'living'[40] and *nozᵉlîm*, 'streaming', and the parallelism of the three images in the space of two colons (4.15ab), contribute to the impression of abundance and breathless proliferation.

The water, which initially hides itself only to burst forth as the life-giving spring in the garden of the woman, never again entirely disappears from view. It is implicit in the description of her lover's hair which is drenched with the dew in 5.2 and is explicit in her description of his eyes in 5.12. They are likened to doves precariously balanced on 'streams of waters', an image which suggests the energetic, even violent course of the melted snows through narrow ravines. The noun used here, *'apiqê* (5.12b), comes from a verb, only used in the *hithpael*, meaning 'to force, to compel, to restrain oneself'. Here it describes the

---

40. The dispute between Isaac and the herdsmen of Gerar over the well of living water that Isaac's servants dig (Gen. 26.19) highlights the vital nature of the commodity to a desert people. It was its life-sustaining quality which made it such an appropriate metaphor for God (Jer. 2.13; 17.13). The image is full of movement; the expression 'living water' everywhere in the Old Testament designates fresh or running water (Lev. 14.5-6, 40-52; Num. 19.17).

channel which confines the waters that vigorously pass through it.[41]

The gathering momentum associated with water imagery reaches a climax in 8.7 where love encounters and survives the onslaught of mighty waters and torrential floods:

> Mighty waters cannot quench love,
> no river can sweep it away.

It is also the point where natural images take on a mythological colouring, as has been demonstrated by May (1955) and Tromp (1969). May directs us to Canaanite mythology, to the conflict between Baal and Yam in which the storm god emerges triumphant over the sea. He suggests that a parallel myth exists in Hebrew mythology as regards Yahweh's power to save. The expression *mayim rabbîm* of 8.7 is often used in this context.[42] Less frequent is *neharot*, 'rivers',[43] which parallels *mayim rabbîm* in 8.7c and which is an alternative name for Yam in the conflict between himself and Baal (*KTU* 1.2, I, 22, 27, 30, 34, 32; *KTU* 1.2, III, 7, 9, 16, 21). It is therefore likely that the *mayim rabbîm* and *neharot* of 8.7 would have been understood by a Hebrew audience not only as natural images but in terms of mythology.

Tromp (1969: 64-65) presses the issue further. He cites instances in the Old Testament where these mighty waters (Ps. 18.4-5, 16; Job 33.22) and rivers (Jon. 2.5) are the domain not only of chaos but also of death. The intention of the statement (8.7), that love will not let mighty waters or floods triumph over it, must then be to reinforce the impact of the first declaration, namely that love is strong as death (8.6c-d). This declaration is openly mythological for it echoes the phrase 'Mot is strong' in the sixth tablet of the Ugaritic myth (*KTU* 1.6, VI, 20). In 8.6 love, the most powerful of primordial forces in the universe, challenges this and is victorious.[44] It is no coincidence that 8.6-7, in which nature takes on the full colouring of mythology, is the climax of the Song.

It is also significant that just as the language of wealth and splendour is subverted at the last moment to describe the immeasurable worth of

41. The use of the noun in Job 6.5 as an image of the treachery of friends expresses well this violence.

42. Hab. 3.15; 2 Sam. 22.17; Ps. 18.16; 29.3; Jer. 51.13.

43. Hab. 3.8; Ps. 93.3-4.

44. Mot is not a deity to whom worship is addressed but rather a primordial entity, the personification of death (Gibson 1979: 164). On the basis of parallelism, Sheol too may be personified here, as indeed it is elsewhere in the Old Testament (Prov. 1.12; Isa. 5.14; Hab. 2.5; see Murphy 1990: 91).

love, so likewise with regard to water imagery, there is a decisive shift in its usage in the final verses. Whereas up to 8.7 water imagery accompanies and describes the growth of love, in 8.7 it ceases to be a positive element and becomes the foil against which love reveals itself to be a fire whose flames these mighty waters can never entirely quench.[45] Love has again broken the limits of the language used to describe it and shows all imagery to be at best tentative, metaphorical. Water has in the end given way to fire (8.6ef) in the attempt to express its power.

The sections of the chapter devoted to nature imagery have been organized in such a way as to convey an ever-increasing density of metaphorical transformation. Flowers, fruit and trees constitute, at a first level, a harmonious backcloth to the relationship. The signs of spring which everywhere appear in the external world are at once a spur to the lovers' already kindled desire and are to some extent the projection of this longing. At a second level, the ripening process which transforms the burgeoning flowers into fruit is a metaphor for a love fully grown. Wine consequently becomes a metaphor for the intimacy of love-making, just as the ripened pomegranate becomes an image of the woman's breasts which she offers to her lover. At a third level, the images of flowers, fruit and trees find their focus in the woman who is described as a garden. Henceforth, she is everywhere present in a world in spring. To the symbolic dimensions of the image we shall return.

Fauna too call forth certain reactions in the lovers; the call of the turtledove is a sign of spring and the little foxes are a warning to beware of the enemies of love. For the most part, however, animals and birds are seen through the prism of the woman; it is her physique as described in the *waṣfs* which gives us access to the details of the Palestinian countryside. Certain motifs are applied to the two lovers in different ways; he is often described as a gazelle or young deer, the very same image used to describe her breasts. The image of the dove undergoes similar transformations, reinforcing both the unity and individuality of

---

45. Though the declaration in 8.6 that 'love is strong as death' is the only one to be openly mythological, the god Rešep may be alluded to in the phrase *rešapeha rišpê 'eš* in the same way that Nahar and Yam are secondary allusions in 8.6. In Ps. 76.4 *rišpê kašet* refer to the fiery arrows which God destroys. Here, shafts of fire are a metaphor for the power of love. As already suggested in the section devoted to *Regal Imagery*, images of war are frequently associated with love in the ancient world. Pope (1977: 670) cites the example of Cupid with his arrows.

the lovers by means of homogeneity and variety of language. The motif of the gazelle, moreover, reappears in the adjuration, easing the passage of a didactic refrain in a lyrical meditation upon love.

Pastoral imagery to an extent draws on the imaginative fields of the preceding sections, both flora and fauna. In this there is considerable metaphorical layering, as increasingly delicate readings suggest themselves on the basis of *sous-entendu* and innuendo arising from previous associations. There is at least one pastoral scene which can be read literally, 1.7-8. Otherwise, either previous associations or the present context alert us to the possibility of a metaphorical reading. It is the context which is decisive in 2.16, for example. On the other hand, it is previous associations that are important in 6.2-3.

I have already alluded to the vine-wine continuum, by means of which different aspects of love are explored using images from the same basic imaginative field. The ripening vines are part of the spring scene and constitute an invitation to love. Wine, on the other hand, evokes the intimacy of love-making, blending easily with the oils and scents and the luxurious apparel of the court. As part of this same imaginative network, the vineyards of Ein-Gedi are cited. On other occasions, however, it is strongly suggested that the vineyard is symbolic, a figure of the woman herself. The symbol relates to her relations with the external world, as represented by her brothers. It is at this point too that the narrativity of the Song once more becomes apparent, in the contrast between before and after, in the woman's progress from enslavement to freedom.

The image of the garden parallels that of the vineyard and yet diverges significantly from it. It also becomes a symbol of the woman, not in relation to the external world, but in relation to her lover. To this garden her lover comes to eat (5.1), for she is both the place and the means of return to a paradise urgently sought after by him. It is no coincidence that the image takes on its fully symbolic dimensions at the midpoint of the Song, for if she represents the beauties of the natural world (flowers, fruit, trees, spices, scents and even water) she is also at the centre of it. Henceforth the edges are untidy, for subsequent references to gardens may or may not be intended to be metaphorical. The effect of this powerful symbolic use of the image at the midpoint of the Song is precisely to open up the possibility of co-existing layers of meaning.

As regards the motif of the vineyard, we noted a marked contrast between before and after, lending once more a degree of narrativity to the Song. As regards the garden, this narrative element is contained in the extended metaphor of 4.10–5.2, telling of the gradual opening of the garden to the woman's lover. Finally, as regards water imagery, by contrast a minor motif, we noted a clear progression throughout the Song: water imagery mirrors the growth of love up until the point when the woman is ready to reflect upon love and declare its power. At this point water imagery ceases to be a positive element and becomes instead the foil against which love reveals its strength.

Chapter 4

IMAGES IN SPACE AND TIME

Time, Timing and Timelessness

The aim of this section is to explore the treatment of time in the Song and to consider the paradoxical relationship between a concern for timeliness and the atmosphere of timelessness which persists throughout. In so doing I aim to uncover something of the dynamic of the Song, a key to understanding how the images work together.

The concern for right timing is most clearly seen in the lovers' anticipation of spring, for the sensuous blossoming which characterizes this season mirrors the awakening of love which they sense in themselves, a phenomenon already alluded to in our discussion of nature imagery, but which deserves more detailed consideration here. In 2.8 the woman hears the voice of her lover as he bounds over the hills to seek her out. On arriving at her window he pleads with her to 'arise' and 'come away' on the grounds that spring is making itself known not only in their own land (2.12c) but indeed throughout the whole earth (2.12a). The urgency of his appeal rests on two factors.

First, the seven colons of 2.11-13 depend on the single conjunction *kî* which establishes a direct relationship between the time for love and the arrival of spring. Second, these colons mirror the steady progress of the season, from the passing of the winter rains towards the end of January to the ripening of the figs in mid-June. The verb *ng'* (2.12b) and the noun *'t* (2.12b) also contribute to the sense of urgency, for the verb *ng'* has the primary meaning 'touch' or 'reach' (used of time in Est. 3.1 and Neh. 7.73) and the noun *'t* is commonly used of the right time for something (for example in Jer. 5.24, Deut. 11.14, Hos. 2.11, Ps. 1.3 and Prov. 15.23).

Onomatopoeia and alliteration also enhance the vigour of the description. In particular, the alliteration of *nun* and *sadhe* in 2.12a sustains the onomatopoeic quality of the initial noun *hannissanîm*, for the freshness of these first spring flowers is conveyed not only by the double meaning of the root *nṣṣ*, 'sparkle' or 'blossom', but also by the combination of letters which make it up, the quality of which is sharp and brittle, like the dazzling appearance of the tiny spring flowers themselves.

The woman accepts her lover's invitation obliquely, using the language with which he has so recently wooed her, that is the language of spring. She does not refer to their relationship directly, but by means of the first person plural suffix implicitly associates herself and her lover with the vineyards now in bloom (2.15). Her concern that the blossoming vines should not be spoilt is a tacit acknowledgment that the time is right. Indeed her appeal to catch the foxes which would damage the vineyards is full of anticipation.

If her lover quickly responds to the new growth with an invitation to the woman to join him in the blossoming countryside in 2.10-15, in 6.11-12 he is rather more ponderous. He simply goes down to the nut orchard to see the spring. There, love takes him by surprise. 6.12 is extremely obscure. Enough sense can be made of the first colon however to suggest that it refers to the power of love to overcome solitude and to transport the lover to his beloved's side.[1]

A third passage, 7.11-12, draws on the theme and vocabulary of 2.11-13, 15 and 6.11-12. Now it is the woman who speaks. She addresses her lover directly and proposes that they leave together for the country. The first person plural form of the four verbs *neṣe'*, *nalînâ*, *naškîmâ* and *nir'eh* stresses a new reciprocity on the part of the lovers—no longer is he required to coax her out of hiding (cf. 2.14) nor is she required to meditate upon an absent lover (cf. 6.11), but together they go out into the countryside to consummate their love. Moreover, it is she who takes the initiative. In contrast to 2.10-15 is the fact that spring is not the catalyst for their meeting. Rather, signs of spring are sought to ratify their already kindled desire for one another. In this 7.11 parallels 6.11, though in 6.11 the male lover seems unaware of the significance of his actions.

Not only does the advent of spring confirm that the time for love has come but it also provides the setting for the lovers' meeting. The description of spring comes to a climax in the woman's promise that it is 'there' that she will give him her love (7.13e). No sooner has spring been invoked and the promise made, than scented mandrakes and delicious fruits appear around their door (7.14). Images of spring have yielded to images of late summer and autumn in anticipation of the

---

1. For a discussion of 6.12, see p. 30, n. 16.

union. The climactic nature of the woman's statement is reinforced by the verb *ṣpn*, for the fruits which deck their doorway are fruits which have been lain aside for the purpose.

Not only does spring stimulate the lovers' longing for each other but the lovers themselves are characterized by the freshness of spring; she is compared to a spring flower, perhaps a crocus or an asphodel, in 2.1, and he is a bundle of henna blossom in her arms in 1.14. Even more so, the lovers are characterized by the plenitude of the ripening season; she delights in eating his fruit, the fruit of the apple tree (2.3), her cheeks are the halves of a pomegranate (4.5), she is an orchard of pomegranates and other delicious fruits (4.16), her navel is like a pile of wheat encircled by water-lilies (7.3), her breasts are like a bunch of dates (7.8) and like clusters of the vine, and her breath like the scent of apples (7.9). She promises him spiced wine, the juice of her pomegranates (8.2) and he comes to her, 'his garden', to gather myrrh and spice (5.1). Spring growth celebrates the birth of love and anticipates its fulfilment. The world in spring mirrors the lovers' happiness and stimulates their desire. Ripening fruits, on the other hand, are the invisible fruits of a love full-grown. They describe the plenitude each finds in the other and represent the gift which they are ready to make of themselves. Spring and summer thus fuse and blend, for the life cycle of plants has become a metaphor of the fulfilment of natural instincts.

Timing continues to be important in the Song. We see it in the woman's desire to know where her lover lies down at noon (1.7), in her desire to go out early into the vineyards (7.12), in the repetend not to awaken love before it is ready (3.5; 8.4) and in the episode beginning in 5.2 in which bad timing provokes a series of disastrous events. This apparent precision however masks an underlying ambiguity as regards time.

Consider, for example, the woman's dismissal of her lover in 2.17 and 8.14. Timing here is of the essence, yet we are unable to determine whether her lover is banished until sunset or sunrise.[2] We do not know therefore whether the meeting takes place during the night or the day. The difficulty is in deciding whether the fleeing of the shadows refers to the shadows which were visible during the day and which disappear

2. Not only is there ambiguity as regards time, but there is ambiguity also as regards space in so far as the command *sob* in 2.17 may mean 'return' or 'turn aside'. It may be that in 2.17 she is not asking him to flee (cf. 8.14) but to come to her. If the verb is interpreted thus then the 'mountains of Bether' become a symbol of herself.

with the coming of nightfall or whether the phrase is a metaphor for the passing of night and the breaking of a new day. Shadows are used in the former sense in Ps. 102.1 and in Ps. 109.23 and in the latter in Jer. 6.4. The reference to the breathing of the day does not help to resolve the dilemma. It could refer either to the cool of the evening after the heat of the day or to the cool of the morning before the heat rises. The main thing is that the lovers understand each other. It is perhaps only we who lack the vital piece of information.

The night search of 3.1-5 has caused similar confusion. The woman recounts how night after night she lay in her bed, longing for her lover, and how one night she decided to get up and go in search of him. The little sketch rapidly draws our attention to her tenderness and to her courage. Her love for him is such that she will risk all for him. Some (Budde, Delitzsch, Gordis) have thought that the story which unfolds does not correspond to actual experience. Rather, the fact that the story begins in the woman's bed and continues with odd behaviour on her part suggests that she may actually be recounting a dream. In a dream, anything is possible.

The narrative of 5.2–6.3 has likewise provoked discussion. Some have suggested that the opening words 'I slept, but my heart was awake' indicates that the words which follow belong to the realm of dream experience (Budde, Freehof, Gordis, Murphy). It is possible, however, that the phrase simply refers to the attentiveness of the woman to her lover even as she sleeps. Not wholly unconscious, she is ever ready for his coming. This is the opinion of Fox (1985: 123). He cites Eccl. 2.23 as another example of such restlessness. The subject of that verse is the one who toils: 'even at night his heart does not lie down'.

Our uncertainty as to whether these passages belong to the realm of dreams or to that of waking reality betrays our uneasiness in the face of temporal and spatial sequences which begin abruptly and have indeterminate endings. That is why it is convenient for Freehof (1948–49) to claim that the Song as a whole is a series of dream sequences. Read thus, the disorder which characterizes the Song 'makes sense' (Pope 1977: 511).

Even if one cannot tell whether the Song belongs to the dreamworld or to waking reality, it may certainly be described as dreamlike, on account of the rapid shifts which are evident from one verse to another. These are inexplicable in terms of objective reality for they disrupt any storyline which might otherwise establish itself. Instead they create an emotional continuum, tracing the way in which joy is endlessly lost and restored in the perpetual search for the loved one. It is love's logic which they, in oneiric fashion, reveal. It is the movement described by Fox (1985: 225) as a 'meandering river' and by Cook (1968: 21) as a circle of 'seeking and finding'. In his words:

> From beginning to end the lovers go from seeking each other to finding each other. But this action does not move in a straight line from separation to union; it leaps in impulsions of voiced desire, from anticipated joy to actualised joy and back again. Any speech may find itself anywhere on the circle of seeking and finding.

Given this itinerary in which the same experiences are endlessly repeated, timelessness overwhelms but does not totally suppress time. A concern for time survives in the urgent longing of the lovers for each other. It is also evident in the timely declaration of love's power (8.6), a declaration which falls at the end of the Song as a comment upon the birth and growth of love. Otherwise, however, sequentiality is subordinate to psychological reality, to the tides of emotion described above. Moreover the ever-shifting perspectives compel the reader to give up the task of distinguishing between the real and the imaginary, the actual and the hoped for, for it becomes apparent that the lovers are capable of experiencing past, present and future with equal intensity.

This was first noted in the section concerning the daughters of Jerusalem. There, it was argued that their presence helps to make the past present. Sometimes, also, private dialogue later appears to belong to past experience, as in 2.1-3, where dialogue between the lovers quickly takes on the character of a narrative (2.4).

It is equally possible, however, that what appears to be reported speech may in fact belong to the future, as for example in 2.8-15, when the woman describes the coming of her lover and his summons to her. It may be that this dialogue is not a memory but rather a fantasy.

For the most part, however, the lovers address each other directly. Indeed the woman's lover strives to bring her back to this immediacy whenever, as in 1.12-14, she begins to take the path of fantasy and to speak of him in the third person. His words are always direct. There are only a few occasions (2.2; 6.9-12) where he does not address her as 'you'. Even the woman's fantasies and memories are occasioned by the desire for his presence, however. The shifts which take place in the course of certain sequences are all directed to this end.

References to particular days and particular times fit into this general pattern. The description of Solomon's wedding (3.6-11), as already suggested, is a metaphor of the male lover's delight in his noble bride. The little sister's betrothal day (8.8), by contrast, belongs not to an idealized past but to an imagined future. It at once hints at the perpetuity of love, which is already present in the next generation, and serves as a pretext pointing to the tension between choice and destiny. Neither event locates the Song in actual time or space. Both are subordinate to psychological reality, to the relationship which is the subject of the Song. The motif of the wedding or betrothal day serves an additional literary purpose in so far as it brings together two imaginative fields which have been important throughout, namely those of regality and family life.

Day and night succeed each other in the same manner that absence gives way to presence in the Song. In addition, they gather around them a series of associations pertinent to the lovers and to their great love. Night is particularly associated with intimacy, for it is then that she goes out in search of him (3.1-5; 5.6) and that he comes to her door (5.2), his head 'drenched with dew', his locks wet 'with the damp of the night'. The verb *lyn*, literally to 'spend the night', is used as a metaphor of the security he feels in her embrace (1.13) and in anticipation of their departure to the countryside (7.11). Night is also associated with the dream-world which the longing for such a meeting provokes. We have already discussed the problem as regards 3.1 and 5.2. If night is the time of greatest intimacy, it is however also the time of greatest vulnerability and of danger. It is the time when the woman suffers at the hands of the nightwatchmen (5.7) and the time when Solomon's litter is most vulnerable to attack from the 'terrors of the night' (3.8).[3]

As regards the day, the early morning is associated with their antici-pated encounter (7.12), while the harshness of the sun, and most especi-ally the noon-day sun, accompanies social disapprobation. It is the scorching sun causing her blackness which is the reason for the contemptuous stares of the daughters of Jerusalem (1.6). It is also the noon-day sun which engenders in the woman both the hope that she

---

3. Krauss (1936: 323-30) testifies to the belief that supernatural powers endangered couples on their wedding night. He points to the story told in Tob. 3.7ff. about the woman who lost seven husbands to the demon Asmodeus before the marriage could be consummated. Though there is little information about such demons in the Old Testament, *Sources Orientalis* 8 (1971): 101-42 describes three demons known in Babylonia, each of which operates at night (cf. *Apoc. Bar.* 10.8; Mk 1.3; 5.2).

may find her love (1.7) and the fear that she may fall into the hands of his shepherd companions instead (1.7de).

Most often however the Song is sung on the threshold of day and night, so rapid is the passage from one event to another. The ambiguous repetend, 'Until the day breathes and the shadows flee' (2.17; 4.16) contributes to this sensation. It is significant that an abbreviated form of this motif marks the temporary conclusion of the Song (8.14). The image of the gazelle on the mountains is just enough to suggest that the ending is but a pause in the Song's movement.

One further aspect remains, namely the theme of awakening. It is most prominent in the adjuration 'Do not arouse or stir up love until it is ready' which appears three times altogether in the Song (2.7; 3.5; 8.4). If love is not to be aroused aforetime, so life-transforming a process is it, nevertheless the woman, when her time comes, calls on the winds to awaken them (4.16). The same verb '*wr* is used here. Henceforth, she cannot sleep. Even as she rests at night, her heart is awake, '*er*. Her warning therefore is to be taken seriously, for love itself is an awakening. This is the implication of her presence at her lover's birth (8.5). No sooner had he entered the world than she awoke ('*orartîka*) him to love, for she has indeed loved him from the beginning.

Images in Space

In the course of this section three main issues arise. First, there is the relationship between the lovers and their environment, and the instability of spatial relationships. Second, there is the association of the lovers with particular places. Third, there is the use of space as a mirror of their desire for each other. Finally, topographical references will be considered.

Space, like time, is primarily psychological, for the lovers' perception of their environment is always determined by their love and longing for each other. The countryside, its vineyards and open hills is often used as a foil on to which the lovers project their feelings, yet it never has any autonomy apart from the lovers' preoccupation with each other. In contrast to the objectivity of the Psalmist in his description of nature,[4] in the Song this external world is drawn into the subjectivity of the lovers so as to be the mirror of their emotional life; signs of spring become signals for the fulfilment of natural instincts and the blossoming vines and fruit trees reflect the delight the lovers discover in each other.

4.   See Lewis 1958.

Throughout the Song scenes shift and fuse with oneiric ease, for the action is not located primarily in the diverse milieux of the Song but in the dialogue of the lovers and in their quest to praise and honour one another. City streets and intimate interiors, the open countryside and its vineyards and gardens, the spacious desert and the awesome distant hills are all called upon in order to illuminate, in different ways, something of this great love. Thus it is that one environment quickly gives way to another, as is evident in the very first verses of the Song (1.2-8).

The Song begins with the evocation of a courtly scene (1.2-4). As the woman turns from her lover to address the daughters of Jerusalem directly, however (1.5-6), so the courtly scene which has been so lightly sketched is increasingly eclipsed. The king and his adoring female entourage, the wines and costly unguents, all of which contribute to the evocation of a courtly milieu, all cede to an exploration of family tensions focusing on the question of property and the role of the woman in the upkeep of the family vineyards (1.5-6). In the course of these verses a movement away from the city takes place. A pastoral scene, corresponding to the outer limits of the civilized world, is the term of this trend (1.7-8). In 1.9-11, however, courtly imagery returns when the woman's lover compares her to a 'mare of the chariotry of Pharaoh'. So it continues throughout the Song.

Double entendre introduces a note of ambiguity into the significance of certain places, particularly the garden and the vineyard, both of which become symbolic of the lovers, and particularly of the woman. As regards the motif of the garden, the more this motif becomes part of the love language of the lovers, the less overt the intended meaning. Whereas in 4.12 the woman is directly compared to a garden by means of an extended metaphor, thereafter the allusion is much more discreet. A number of elements in 6.2-3 alert the reader to the possibility of *double entendre*. First of all, the male lover is said to descend to 'his garden', a phrase reminiscent of 4.16 in which the woman invites him to come to 'his garden' and eat its 'luscious fruits'. The garden referred to in 4.16 is clearly herself. Secondly, the language of grazing among water-lilies is already associated with love-making, principally on account of the imagery of 4.5 in which her breasts are likened to suckling fawns feeding on water-lilies. Thirdly, the motif of gathering is used only once elsewhere, in connection with the male lover's delight in his garden, the heroine of the Song (5.1). There, he 'gathers' myrrh and spice. Finally, the likening of the woman not only to a single garden but to a multiplicity of gardens in 4.12–5.1 invites the reader to consider this same sudden proliferation to be an indication of the liveliness of the woman also in 6.2c. No direct identification is ever explicitly made, however, with the result that the symbolic nuances remain subliminal. Eros pervades the entire landscape which the lovers inhabit, just as it stimulates all their actions and guides their perceptions of each other.[5] The lack of definition of symbolic meanings as regards certain places, garden or vineyard, suggests that the entire universe is permeated by an atmosphere of love.

Nowhere is the instability of setting more clearly evident than in the *wasfs* or descriptive songs (4.1-7; 5.10-16; 6.4-10; 7.2-10a), for in these songs it is the body of the loved one that is the point of coherence of a number of diverse settings and of a multiplicity of images. In the *wasf* of 4.1-7, for example, the slopes of Gilead and the valley below are mentioned in 4.1, whereas the scene is the tower of David, presumably in Jerusalem, in 4.3. In 4.5 the setting is again the countryside, namely the shady pools where gazelles feed on delicious water-lilies. Interspersed are images drawn from a number of milieux—scarlet thread from the weaver's shuttle (4.3), pomegranates from the orchard (4.2) and shy doves (4.1) such as those found in the covert of the cliff (2.14). Each of these coheres in the self-contained idyllic world which comes into view whenever the lover contemplates his beloved. Indeed each aspect of her body in turn suggests another of its beauties.

Characteristic of these *wasfs* is the fact that the images chosen to correspond to particular parts of the body are more memorable than the referents themselves on account of the originality of the imagery and the extent to which the metaphors are elaborated.[6] This is another ruse by means of which the idyllic world which the lovers inhabit appears to be more stable than it is. Indeed there are occasions when the images used to describe the loved one do actually take on a life of their own and seek to identify the lovers with the world they inhabit. In 7.8 for example, the

5.   Translated 'night after night', this is a further example of a plural of generalization (cf. 1.4, 9, 17; 2.9 etc.).

6.   In the *wasf* of 4.1-5 for example, the imagery which describes different parts of the body is more or less elaborate. The imagery which describes her teeth (4.2) extends over four colons, that which describes her neck (4.4) and breasts (4.5) over three colons and that which describes her lips (4.3a) and mouth (4.3b) over one colon only. As regards the more highly developed metaphors, active verbs (4.1e, 2b) or participles (4.4bc, 5c) accompany them. The referent in each case is simply placed in a nominal clause.

male lover compares the woman to a palm tree on account of her formidable stature. From then on, she actually becomes a palm tree which he endeavours to climb (7.9).

Not only is the world visible in the loved one but it is also touched, tasted, felt and heard, for if the charm of the loved one appeals to the senses, then sensuality also pervades the world by means of which the lovers describe each other. The sense which dominates varies from image to image. In 4.1c-f, for example, the image depends principally on vision in order to communicate the vivacity of the woman's head of curls. In 4.5 on the other hand, in an image which also conveys the male lover's longing to be near to her breasts, the senses of sight, touch and perhaps taste are called upon. The extended image of the garden (4.12–5.1) demonstrates most clearly the way in which the world is touched and tasted in the beloved. To her, he comes to feed—on myrrh, milk, wine and honey (5.1).

Another aspect of the highly subjective nature of the Song is the blurring of distinctions between absence and presence, dream and reality. As Ramon Lull so aptly said, 'Whether Lover and Beloved are near or far is all one'.[7] This ambiguity is evident in the very first verses (1.2-4). There, the poet teasingly introduces the motifs of absence and presence, longing and fulfilment which mark the Song. He does so by, among other things, omitting the rubrics necessary to set the verses in time and space.

In 1.2-4 one would be hard pressed to define the situation exactly. 1.2 begins with the woman's longing for her lover whom she addresses first in the third (1.2) and then in the second person (1.2), a distinction which may convey a shift from absence to presence or which may simply be an example of the stylistic technique known as enallage, which is fairly common in poetry (cf. Deut. 32.15; Isa. 1.29; Jer. 22.24; Mic. 7.19). If the former is more accurate, then the question remains as to whether he is actually present to her or whether her longing for him is sufficient to make it seem as if he is. What is actually the case there is no way of knowing.

She continues to praise him in 1.3, claiming that he is also loved by the ladies of the court. In 1.4 and 1.5, she oscillates between seeking his exclusive attention and joining with the other young women in his praise. There is in these verses a bewildering mixture of desiring to be his alone and seeking to highlight his uniqueness by enlisting others in

7.   Cited in Reinhold (ed.) 1947: 261.

his praise. It is impossible to judge whether he does actually accomplish what she hopes he will. The ambiguity is compounded by the verbal form *hebî'anî* which may either be read as the second person masculine *hiphil* perfect with first person suffix, 'he has drawn me', or, more unusually, as a precative perfect, 'Let him bring me'. Such distinctions are in the end useless, for what the poet seeks to convey are two contradictory impulses on the part of the woman, namely to delight in her lover in private and to show him off in public. More profoundly, what the ambiguity alerts the reader to is the paradoxical distinction between absence and presence. Though he is physically absent, her yearning for him is never satisfied. Time and space are indeed psychological; they mark the lovers' mutual love and longing.

This situation repeats itself on numerous occasions throughout the Song. In 2.8, for example, the woman announces the arrival of her lover. The reported speech of 2.10 alerts the reader to the possibility that the episode is a memory relived. So strongly present is he to her, however, that she responds to his call, first with a warning about the little foxes (2.15) and then with a joyous declaration of their mutual belonging (2.16). Finally, in 2.17, she begs him to flee, a statement which suggests that at that moment he is present to her.

Throughout this book, other instances of sudden shifts from absence to presence have been noted. There is the search for her lover in 5.6-7 and her request to the daughters of Jerusalem to help her in the task (5.8). When they respond (6.1) she replies (6.2) that she knows exactly where he is, using such language as to strongly suggest that she is already with him.

Finally there is the repetend, 'His left hand holds my head and his right hand is round me' (2.7; 8.4), which may either be read as indicative, as the fulfilment of longing, or as optative, as an expression of yearning for his presence.

The task of the reader is not to solve these ambiguities as if there were an actual situation or story-line to be discerned. Rather they highlight the interrelationship between absence and presence in the depth of love. Moreover, the ambiguity created by such shifts is most often in favour of the presence of the absent loved one, for hope anticipates the joy of their presence.

While spatial relationships are in a state of permanent flux, it is however possible to discern a pattern in the kinds of places with which each lover is associated. As already noted, the woman is most often associated with images of enclosure or hiddenness. She it is whose lively eyes and ruddy cheeks are sheltered from the direct gaze of her lover by a veil (4.1, 3; 6.7), she too it is who is likened to a shy dove hiding in the mountain-side (2.14) and who is borne in a litter that hides her from view (3.6-11). On three occasions she waits indoors for her lover (2.10-14; 3.1; 5.2-6) and on two occasions she wanders the streets of the city, itself a kind of prison (3.2-3; 5.7). There are also the images of the spring (4.12), the garden (4.12–5.1) and the vineyard (1.6; 8.11-12), each of which is symbolic of her. Even her lover's embrace shelters (2.3) and enfolds her (2.6; 8.3).

The narratives of 2.10-14, 5.2-6 and 3.1-4 are particularly interesting and deserve further attention. First of all it should be remembered that the motif of the youth waiting at his lover's door in 2.10-14 and 5.2b has a very long history. According to Jacobsen (1976: 35) the opening of the door of the bride's house was 'the central ceremony in a Sumerian wedding, which concluded the marriage and immediately preceded its consummation'. It is reflected in the courtship of Dumuzi and Inanna (*ANET*: 639):

> Open the house, my queen, open the house.

The motif also appears in the Egyptian love-song tradition. In the Egyptian love-song cited by Fox (1985: 75), the door is a sign of his lover's indifference:

> As for what she—(my) sister—did to me,
> Should I keep silent to her?
> She left me standing at the door of her house
> while she went inside,
> and did not say to me 'Welcome!'
> but blocked her ears in my night.

The motif appears for the first time in the Song in 2.10-14. The first two colons of 2.8 are extremely terse, conveying the suddenness of her lover's appearance. An exclamation opens each colon as first he is heard (2.8a) and then seen (2.8b). The exclamation 'Behold' (2.9c) and the parallel participle phrases which follow in 2.9c, e, f take the reader by surprise. Indeed the force of the participles is that she scarcely notices him arrive. The time taken to register his coming is longer than he needs, for he is already standing at her door, wooing her to come to his side (2.9).

The motif appears for a second time in 5.2, here at the heart of a mini-narrative. The *récit* begins with the woman lying, as before, in bed (cf. 3.1). Whereas in 3.1 she could not settle, however, but got up to seek her lover, in 5.2 she is already half asleep even though subconsciously she is attentive to his coming:

I slept, but my heart was awake.

The scene is scarcely set (5.2a) when the action begins with the announcement of the arrival of her lover who, as in 2.9, is initially heard rather than seen (5.2b). As in 2.9 the noun *kôl* alerts the reader to his coming. Whereas in 2.9, however, his approach is described in detail, thereby allowing time for her anticipation to grow and dramatic tension to mount, in 5.2 he arrives without any such warning. Indeed she has barely acknowledged his arrival (5.2b) when his urgent entreaty begins (5.2c):

Open to me,
my sister, my love,
my dove, my perfect one,
for my head is drenched with dew,
my locks[8] with the damp of the night

Even as he addresses her, she hesitates to open to him (5.3):

I had put off my robe,
how could I put it on again?
I had bathed my feet,
how could I dirty[9] them?

The effect of her delay is destructive beyond all her imaginings, however, for her lover grows impatient and attempts unsuccessfully to let himself in, thrusting his hand[10] into the keyhole in the absence of a key to unlock the door.[11]

---

8. *q^{e}wuṣṣôtay* is a *hapax legomenon*, the sense of which has been ascertained on the basis of the parallelism with *šerro'sî*, 'my head'.

9. *'atann^{e}pem* comes from the root *ṭnp*, a *hapax legomenon* in the Old Testament. It is attested in Aramaic and Akkadian, meaning 'to soil'.

10. Pope (1977: 517-19) argues that the lover's hand is a euphemism for the phallus and that the image is of coitus. He refers to Isa. 57.8-10 where the term *yad* is used twice in this sense and to the Ugaritic poem 'The Birth of the Beautiful Gods', where El's 'hand' is said to be 'as long as the sea' (*KTU* 1.23 i 34-35). Given that the context is the sacred marriage rite (De Moor 1987: 117), the translation 'phallus' seems appropriate there. Lastly, the term is used in this sense in the Manual of Discipline at Qumran (1257.13) where a penalty is to be paid by the man who reveals

There has been much discussion of 5.4. The phrase *šalaḥ yad* normally means 'to stretch out the hand' and is usually followed by the preposition *'el* or *bᵉ* (Fox 1985: 144). Here however the preposition *min* is used as in Ps. 144.7 and Ezek. 10.7. In these two passages it designates the withdrawal of the hand, suggesting that the phrase should also be translated in this sense in 5.4a. 5.4b would therefore convey the woman's disappointment. As in Isa. 16.11, where the same verb is used, it becomes part of a phrase which expresses pain.

Apart from Goulder (1986) and Gordis (1974), this interpretation has not received many adherents, for it does violence to the dramatic development of the sequence. It does so by placing the emphasis solely upon the withdrawal of his hand which becomes tantamount to an announcement of his departure. Consequently, when she finally gets up to open the door (5.6), she already half expects him to be gone. The four colons of this verse which describe her decision to get up and to open the door to him are thereby made redundant, for the reader is warned aforetime of his change of heart.

A variation of this interpretation is the suggestion that the preposition *min* cryptically conveys the lover's change of mood as he puts his hand to the door and withdraws it again in a fit of pique, suddenly annoyed at her hesitancy which he interprets—rightly or wrongly—as teasing which has gone too far.

The advantage of this reading is the dramatic tension it creates, for the verse constitutes both the climax of his attempts to communicate with her (which began in 5.2) and the turning point in his advances. Hence, when she responds in 5.5 it is with anxiety and desire. Both are kindled simultaneously as he puts his hand to the door and takes it away in the same movement.

Possible though this interpretation is, it does not however bring out the full impact of the failed meeting in the way that is possible if 5.4 is translated positively, 'My beloved thrust his hand in through the key-hole'.

---

his nakedness by putting out his 'hand' from beneath his clothing. Even if *yad* does have this meaning in certain contexts, this cannot be the primary meaning of the term in 5.4. The poet teases the reader with the suggestiveness of his language yet he is careful to avoid making direct references to coitus.

11. The term *haḥor*, literally 'the hole', does not make it clear what kind of aperture is involved. It may be a keyhole large enough for the hand (Pope 1977: 518) or it may be an opening through which the door may be opened from outside (Gordis 1974: 90).

Delitzsch (1875) first defended this translation. On the basis of 2.9, he pointed out that the perspective of the speaker is all important. On both occasions the woman is inside and relates how her lover sought to communicate with her from outside; he peers in *from* the vantage point of window and lattice (2.9) and seeks access to her chamber by means of the keyhole (5.4). Alternatively there is the argument of Pope (1977: 518) who, on the basis of Ugaritic usage, claims that the prepositions *be* and *min* are interchangeable in Hebrew. Thus it is that many commentators (Fox, Murphy, Keel, Pope) translate the preposition *min* by 'into' or 'through'.

This interpretation lends itself to the assumption that it is a question not so much of a lovers' tiff but of the failure of the lovers to communicate in the same way. He seeks to communicate with her through word and action, first by knocking at her door (5.2b) and then by calling to her (5.2c-f). She, on the other hand, is unable to respond to him other than emotionally—with a wakeful heart (5.2a) and with the coy reserve that delays their meeting (5.3). The events which follow, his precipitate departure (5.6) and her search for him by night (5.6de), are therefore the direct result of the difference between them.

In the light of this irony 5.4 plays a major part, for his attempts to communicate with her culminate in his decision to turn away in spite of the fact that inside she is moved by unprecedented emotion for him. The Hebrew puts it much more strongly, 'My heart turned over'. The choice of the verb is surely deliberate. Unable to call to him directly or to open the door, her whole being nevertheless responds to him with inarticulate emotion. At this very moment he reckons his attempts to have failed.

The irony of these events is emphasized by the fact that by the time the woman does finally get up to open the door to her lover, the drama has already moved definitively into the realm of past experience, as is indicated by the consistent use of the perfect tense 'I arose', 'my hands dripped', 'I opened', 'my love had turned', 'I swooned' in 5.6-7. Events are no longer in her control even although she is, at last, the principal actor. Indeed from the moment he put his hand to the door (5.4) events move her inexorably towards her fate.

In 5.5 the woman acts decisively for the first time, as is conveyed by the forceful personal pronoun *'anî* which accompanies the first person singular perfect verb *qamtî*, 'I arose'. The word order of 5.5a is straightforward, conveying the directness of her intentions. Her emotion is betrayed however immediately thereafter by her hands which drip with myrrh. The elaboration of this image over three colons (5.5b-d) gradually delays the opening of the door and conveys the anxious anticipation of the woman, for whom every moment of separation increases her longing. Indeed her movement to the door is described wholly in emotional terms, in terms of myrrh which flows from her fingers as a sign of her love and longing:

> I arose to open to my love
> and my hands dripped with myrrh,
> my fingers ran with liquid myrrh
> upon the handle of the latch.
> I opened to my love...

The climactic statement of 5.6a to which this imagery leads is remarkable for its directness. The simplicity of the statement 'I opened to my love' (5.6a) draws attention to its importance. The questions she put to herself in 5.3 and the detailed description of her reaction to his calling in 5.4-5 have all delayed the immediate response he demanded in 5.2. The question now is whether the time taken by these reflections has exceeded the limits of his patience. The use of the verb *pth*, 'to open', at each key moment in the drama—in his entreaty (5.2), at the moment of her decision (5.5) and now in her fulfilment of his request (5.6)— heightens the tension, for the distance in the narrative between the entreaty *pithî-lî* (5.2c) and her response *patahti 'anî* (5.6a) makes the reader all too aware of the danger of her being too late.

Sadly, happenings in the psyche run according to the same pace as events in the narrative. There is no speeding up of the emotional life in order to keep abreast of the demands without. Hence in spite of the reader's willingness to urge the woman on, it is in fact too late. Her disappointment is expressed in few words (5.6b):

> ...but my love had turned and was gone.[12]

With his disappearance, her life has also 'gone out' (5.6c). There is nothing left at all to her save his departure.

The metaphor of 5.6c works in two ways. On the basis of Gen. 35.18 the expression 'my life went out' seems to refer metaphorically to death. The woman uses the image to proclaim her life void. She is not dead, but she seems to be, hence I have translated the phrase by 'I swooned'. Paradoxically, however, the life that goes out of her, leaving her

---

12. The asyndetic construction *hamaq 'abar* is strongly emphatic.

bewildered and demoralized, finds itself renewed in the search for her lover (5.6d-e). The image of death and devastation becomes temporarily an image of hope, inspiring her to get up and follow her lover wherever he is. The ensuing night search in the city (5.7) takes us beyond the motif of the woman waiting indoors for her lover. It also introduces the next topic, namely the relationship of the woman to the city.

The woman's failure to make contact with her lover either by calling (5.6e) or seeking him (5.6d) is compounded by the fact that although she is unsought, the city guards find her (5.7). These faceless men, the 'keepers of the walls' (5.7e), reinforce the prison-like defenses of the place by circulating therein, imposing a harsh discipline upon strangers. Like the bedchamber, the city is an enclosed, protected place. It does not function in favour of lovers, however, but rather in favour of society, whose interests are sometimes quite different. It is not clear of what they accuse the woman, whether of harlotry or of adultery, but their violence towards her, beating her, wounding her and tearing off her veil (5.7), leave her in no doubt that the flight of a single woman through the streets at night is unacceptable. The episode is reminiscent of the night flight of the woman in Prov. 7.10 and of the warnings given to the young man to be careful to avoid those such as she (Prov. 7.5ff.). The watchmen in the Song presumably act on such advice as this without being able to tell who, or what, she is. The Song however is not written from the perspective of their good intentions but from that of the woman who protests against their violence.

5.7 is constructed in such a way as to emphasize her vulnerability and the violence of the regime. The verse opens with the announcement of her capture; rather than find her lover, she herself is found, $m^e\!sa'\hat{u}ni$, literally, 'they found me'. Her captors are then named (5.7ab). Their lengthy title, 'the watchmen who go about in the city', testifies to their role which is surveillance and defence. The three verbs ($hikk\hat{u}ni$, $p^e\!sa'\hat{u}n\hat{\imath}$, $nas^{e\prime}\hat{u}$) which one after another describe their cruelty—'they beat me', 'they wounded me', 'they stripped me of my mantle'—draw attention to the helplessness of the woman, while the new title given to them, 'the keepers of the walls' (5.7e), gives authority to their actions.

The city is associated with the woman also in 3.1-4. There, the tone is quite different. As in 2.8-10 and 5.2-6, the woman waits indoors for her lover. Indeed the plural *blylwt*, literally 'in the nights', suggests that she has often lain in bed yearning for him (3.1). One night, the night described in the Song, she decides to go in search of him (3.2). Once begun, the search dominates the narrative. It does so by means of a number of key motifs combined in a rapid succession of events. To this intensely repetitive sequence, every extraneous detail is sacrificed:

> Night after night on my bed
> I *sought my true love*
> I *sought* him but did not *find* him
> I said, 'I will arise now and go the rounds of the city,
> through the streets and squares,
> *seeking my true love*'.
> I *sought* him but could not find him.
> The watchmen *found* me
> as they made their rounds of the city.
> 'Have you seen *my true love*?'
> Scarcely had I passed them
> when I *found my true love*...

Here, it is not elaborate imagery which conveys the woman's longing. Rather it is the momentum of the narrative as it strains relentlessly onward towards the resolution of the search. Only once her lover has been found does the lyrical language reappear. The anticipation of bringing him home to her mother's house brings about this change (3.4):

> I held him, now I will not let him go
> till I bring him to my mother's house,
> to the chamber of her who conceived me.

Though the rigorous demands of narrativity preclude any development of the relationship between the woman and the nightwatchmen, on the basis of their encounter in 3.4, some comment may be made. Both parties rove the city independently, unaware of each other's presence until the watchmen come across her in 3.4. Even then, they only pay attention to each other because they are both roaming the city, which is usually deserted at night. The element of companionship which this affords is, however, cut short by their very different concerns, the watchmen with security, the woman with love. As soon as she sees them, the woman asks the watchmen if they have seen her lover. Their silence conveys either their astonishment or their indifference. The woman, for her part, does not wait for a reply, but passes on to be eventually reunited with her lover, leaving the dialogue with the watchmen unfinished. In this brief and unsatisfactory encounter, two worlds meet for an instant, only to part once more.

One further remark may be made as regards 3.1-4, namely the progressive narrowing of concentric circles as the woman anticipates leaving the city streets (3.2) to bring her lover into the intimacy of her mother's house (3.4d) and bedchamber (3.4e). These motifs were discussed in the section on *Motherhood*.

In the course of this book it has been noted how very often the woman is seen 'inside', inside city walls, behind windows or behind doors. It has also been demonstrated that garden and vineyard are not only enclosed, self-contained places where the lovers frequently go, but that they also become symbolic of the woman. The reader thereby becomes accustomed to associating her with stability and interiority and to observing her lover move to and from where she is. In the section on the *Garden*, I argued for the centrality of the symbol as a means of access to paradise; the woman is not only functionally but symbolically at the heart of the Song.

Sometimes, however, she surprises the reader by being neither 'inside' spatially, nor at the centre in terms of narrative perspective. Occasionally she is seen moving on the margins of the world she dominates, observed by others who remark upon her movements (3.6; 8.5) or summoned by her lover who calls to her to come down from the distant heights of Senir and Hermon (4.8). The introduction of these motifs enables other qualities of the woman, unexplored by images of hiddenness and enclosure, to come to view. Her awesome beauty (3.6) and tender strength (8.5) are disclosed in her emergence from the desert. Her almost mystical otherness is hinted at by her occupation of distant and dangerous mountain peaks (4.8). By reason of their infrequence these images are important.

In 8.5, and perhaps also in 3.6,[13] the woman emerges in dazzling splendour, ascending without warning from an unspecified location in the wilderness. On both occasions her appearance in the desert follows a sequence which culminates in the anticipation of meeting in the intimacy of her mother's house (3.4; 8.2). In each case there is a striking contrast between the seclusion of her maternal home and the open expanses of the desert. The skill of the poet is to be able to use the austerity of the desert landscape in order to bring to light some aspect of the woman which the landscape in spring does not highlight, her awesome beauty in 3.6, her vulnerability in 8.2. She appears suddenly out of nowhere like a mirage in the desert wastes. On both occasions the strangeness of the vision provokes the rhetorical question, 'Who is this?' (3.6; 8.5). The emphasis of the two verses, however, is subtly different. As already

---

13. For a discussion of this possibility, see p. 40.

argued, her emergence from the desert in 3.6 is integrated into a detailed description of the progress of Solomon's litter towards Jerusalem. In 8.5ab, on the other hand, the woman does not ascend from the desert amid pomp and ceremony but simply leans on her lover. Together they emerge from the desert, triumphing, not by means of military might (cf. 3.7-8) but by mutual tenderness, over this the realm of chaos and death (cf. Jer. 4.23).

In both these verses, in contrast to the male lover who descends into his garden (6.2) or to his nut orchard (6.11), the woman ascends from the desert. The destination of this ascent is, in 3.6-11, Jerusalem. In 8.5 the destination is not specified, although the use of the verb *'lh* is reminiscent of the pilgrim's ascent to the holy city (Isa. 2.3; Ps. 24.3; 122.4). These references, explicit and implicit, are surely not coincidental. Are they not intended to direct the reader back to the redactorial centre of the Song, that is, to the city where the woman tells her confidantes, the daughters of Jerusalem, of the events of love?

The other milieu associated with the woman is Lebanon and the northern peaks of Hermon and Amana (4.8).[14] In 4.8 she inhabits these northern peaks, making her an attractive yet most formidable figure. There, she moves among lions and panthers in complete safety, mistress of the domain she inhabits and of all that there is therein.[15] Distant and inaccessible, she holds sway over this awesome landscape, over the margins of the unknown until her lover calls her to be the garden of his delight (4.12ff.). Even as he approaches his garden, however, all the mysterious otherness of Lebanon is rediscovered there, in the scent of her clothes (4.11) and in the intoxicating effect she has on him.[16] As Lebanon is discovered in the garden of the beloved, however, so it loses any hint of menace. On the contrary, associated with the garden, it participates in this symbol of sheer delight. In so doing, it regains

---

14. These are the highest peaks of Palestine. Lebanon rises to a height of 3,083 m, while Hermon, otherwise known as Senir (Deut. 3.9), and Amana constitute the formidable peaks of anti-Lebanon.

15. The formidable aspect of the ancient love goddess Ishtar was depicted in iconography in a similar way. According to Keel (1986: 148) lions and panthers are often associated with her and she is often depicted enthroned upon mountains. Remembrance of the ancient goddess of love and war adds a menacing note to a dramatic backcloth.

16. This is conveyed by the verbal form *libbabtinî* (4.9), which closely resembles the place name *lᵉbanon* (4.8).

something of the paradisaical association it enjoys elsewhere in the Old Testament (Ezek. 31.4, 6).

Unlike the woman, who is most often associated with enclosed, hidden places and only exceptionally with desert and distant mountain range, her lover is most often associated with the freedom of the open spaces, with mountains and hills of relative proximity to her door (2.8). These are not the dangerous heights of Lebanon or Hermon in the north, where wild animals lie in wait, but the hills of Samaria and Judah, the secluded habitat of stag and gazelle. They are places such as Bether (2.17), the modern Bittîr, 17 km from Jerusalem.[17]

Even although her lover never moves too far from the woman's door and even though she does keep a close check on his movements, parting for all that, always creates distance, physical and psychological. Thus it is that his relatively accessible mountain refuge takes on the character of distant mountains, the places where exotic perfumes, myrrh and frankincense have their origin (4.6; 8.14).[18] These could be India or Persia via the spice routes of Arabia. Alternatively, the image may simply refer to the equally distant mountains of the imagination—mountains belonging to the far-off other world from which the lover visits her. It must also be remembered however that myrrh and frankincense are also associated with the woman. Indeed in 4.6 it is perhaps to the woman herself that the motif of the mountain of myrrh and hill of frankincense refers, for his decision to take himself there immediately follows a description of her breasts with which the motif very well accords (4.5, 7a). It may then be that, far from leaving her, he vows to take refuge in her that night. Yet again the reader is astonished by the agility of the poet, by his capacity to raise a doubt in the mind even as he presses his interpretation in a particular direction.

The Song, as has been said many times before, is a perpetual search, a search that is completed only in the finding of the loved one and in the beginning of the search all over again. This ongoing search for communion with the other is expressed largely in spatial terms. It is disclosed in the movement between the two realms occupied by the lovers, inside

17. This is the suggestion made by Carroll (1923–24: 79). Vg, Aquila and Symmachus also consider the form to be a proper name.

18. Indeed Rabin (1973: 205, 219) grounds the motifs of longing in the custom of young men to absent themselves for long periods at a time. The 'mountains of myrrh' are to him the hills of South Arabia to which the absent lover set off in a caravan.

and outside, and in the crossing of the threshold from one to the other. Seeking admission inside and being drawn outside are the two key movements which together define this desire. Predominant is the movement inside, for interior environments are associated with intimacy and a certain privacy. The woman longs to take her lover to the privacy of her mother's house (3.4; 8.2), he draws her to his private chambers (1.4) and his wine house (2.4); and finally, it is to be admitted to the seclusion of her room that he comes to her door in 5.1. The lovers also long for the freedom of the countryside. He comes to her door to draw her out in 2.1 and she expresses the desire to go out into the country with him in 7.12.

The key motif in this dual movement, inside and outside, is the image of the garden, for it comes to embrace both contradictory impulses; he comes to her, his garden, to discover the world recreated in her. Henceforth he sees in the world around him a garden filled with her presence. The motifs of the vineyard and of the hills of Lebanon also participate in this *double entendre* in so far as they are at times the setting for the lovers' dialogue and at other times the images used of the woman herself.

It was suggested in the section on the *Garden* that the crossing of the threshold to enter the garden constitutes the restoration of the unity and the communion of paradise. The Song does not end, however, with the man's entry into the garden and his discovery of its delights. The sudden intrusion of 'friends' in 5.2 breaks the lovers' communion and obliges the search to begin again (5.3). The reader is thereby sharply reminded that this is not the original Eden, a realm of thresholds definitively crossed. It is rather our world, a world of ambiguity where distinctions are continually to be recognized and where freedom is forever to be gained. Eden, like Lebanon, is marked by discord and by danger, yet it continues to hold forth the hope of communion. It is in terms of spatial relationships that this longing is conveyed and the process begun.

In the preceding section I emphasized the role of the setting in pointing up the situation of the lovers and the way in which the Palestinian locale is internalized as a foil to their changing moods. The ancient setting is, however, never drowned out by being internalized. Indeed the psychologizing treatment of particular places depends on close observation and knowledge of specific locations. It is, for example, the ruggedness of the Lebanese mountains which make them an appropriate metaphor for the woman's inaccessibility in 4.8. Topographical references are extremely important, for they contribute to the distinctively Hebrew character of the Song.

Most references to locality direct us to the north, to the hills of Senir, Hermon and Carmel, to the ancient capital of Tirzah and beyond to Lebanon in the far north. Alternatively, we find ourselves in Transjordan, in Gilead, in Heshbon, the capital of Sihon, king of the Amorites or in Kedar, the territory of the war-like descendants of Ishmael. Only exceptionally is reference made to Judah. Ein-Gedi, by the shores of the Dead Sea, and the village of Bether, 12 km from Jerusalem, are its sole representatives. Cursory mention is made of Egypt (1.9) and of Syria (7.4).

Biblical associations with these localities do frequently help in the interpretation of the Song. Ein-Gedi, for example, was both a refuge for royalty (1 Sam. 24) and a well-known garden of dates (2 Chron. 20.2). Ein-Gedi is precisely a place of refuge for the lovers, a refuge which is also a garden of delight.

Biblical references to Kedar help us clarify the imagery of 1.4. There the woman likens herself to the curtains of Solomon and the tents of Kedar. The former evokes the splendour of Solomon's court, while the latter refers to the rude goat-hair tents of the people of Kedar. These people, living in the desert of Transjordan, on the limits of the civilized world (Isa. 42.10; Jer. 2.10), were known to be wealthy on account of their livestock (Jer. 49.27; Ezek. 27.21; Isa. 60) and war-like on account of their descendence from Ishmael (Ps. 120.57; Gen. 16.12). The tribe was thus an unsettling neighbour for Israel and an appropriate image of the woman's marginal position which she so adamantly defends (1.5). The antithetical parallelism of tents and curtains which successfully contrasts two quite different milieux is well known. It is evident in Jer. 10.20, Hab. 3.7 and Jer. 49.28.

Gilead is mentioned in two identical images describing the woman's hair (4.1; 6.5):

> Your hair is like a flock of goats
> moving down Mount Gilead.

The flowing tresses of her hair are likened to lines of black goats as they wend their way down the mountain-side. It is the movement of her hair which the image seeks to convey. There is, however, a darker side to the image, namely a certain compelling attractiveness which emanates from her hair to captivate her loved one.[19] Indeed the image of the woman's hair as bait which her lover cannot resist is a favourite theme of ancient Egyptian love songs:

...her hair is bait
in the trap to ensnare me (Fox 1985: 19).

And again:

With her hair she lassoes me,
with her eye she pulls me in (Fox 1985: 73).

Gilead is an appropriate setting for such an image. It is a mountainous region, east of Jordan, a region which is thickly wooded and teeming with livestock (Mic. 7.14; Jer. 50.19). It is easy to imagine how one could associate such a region with a lively head of hair. Moreover, it is an area on the frontiers of the known world (Isa. 17.2; 32.14; Jer. 6.3), a place whose distance from the centre accords well with the woman's awesome allure.

Sometimes the choice of a particular setting is determined by the suggestiveness of its name. Thus it is that Tirzah, from the root *rṣh*, 'to take pleasure in', is coupled with Jerusalem, the city described as the perfection of beauty in Ps. 50.2 and Lam. 2.5. Both cities proclaim the woman's proud beauty. The fact that they both served for a while as capital cities, Jerusalem in the south and Tirzah in the north, makes them highly suitable for the task. To the evocation of splendour, they bring connotations of royalty and strength and, on account of their location in the mountains, height. It is worth remembering that Heshbon too was a royal city, the capital of the Amorites. Each of these distinguished locations contributes to the grandeur of the heroine.

Of all the places in the Song, Lebanon is among the most frequently mentioned. It is mentioned six times in all, in a variety of different contexts. In 5.15 it is associated with the man. His 'appearance is like Lebanon, choice as the cedars', an image which draws on the reputed strength and grandeur of these Lebanese trees. These are the trees which display God's greatness in Ps. 29.5 and Ps. 104.16 and which were hewn by Solomon's servants in order to build the house of God in

---

19. Not only was hair considered an attribute of female beauty but, as the story of Samson demonstrates, it was considered to be a source of life and strength (Judg. 16.5). Warriors wore their hair loose, no doubt as a sign of their virility (Ps. 68.22; Judg. 5.2).

1 Kgs 5.6 and his own house in 1 Kgs 7.23. These are also the cedars which form the solid framework of his litter in 3.9.

In 4.8, 11 and 15, it is with the woman that Lebanon is associated, first on account of its formidable height and inaccessibility, secondly, on account of the fragrance which emanates from there (Hos. 14.5-7), and lastly, on account of the freshness and vitality of its mountain streams. The woman calls upon each of these aspects in turn; she is awesome as distant Lebanon (4.8), her clothes are pervaded by the suggestion of its exotic scents (4.11) and her youthful enthusiasm for her loved one's embrace finds its expression in its rushing streams.

Lebanon never occupies the foreground in the Song yet it is invoked throughout the Song in relation to both lovers as a symbol of stability, prosperity and romantic exoticism. The allusions of the Hebrew poets to a place of great natural beauty are never far from our mind. We recall the promise to the righteous that 'they will grow like a cedar in Lebanon' (Ps. 92.12) and the promise to Israel that 'his fragrance shall be like Lebanon' (Hos. 14.6). Indeed Hos. 14.5-7 clearly demonstrates the paradisaical dimensions of the motif:

I will be as dew to Israel
he shall blossom as a lily
he shall strike root as the poplar
his roots shall spread out;
his beauty shall be like the olive
and his fragrance like Lebanon.
They shall return and dwell beneath
my shadow
they shall flourish as a garden,
they shall blossom as the vine,
their fragrance shall be like the wine of Lebanon.

Isaiah too (60.13), in his vision of the future glory of Zion, calls upon these same associations:

The glory of Lebanon shall come to you,
the cypress, the plane and the pine,
to beautify the place of my sanctuary;
and I will make the place of my feet glorious.

Remarkable in the Song is the infrequent mention of Jerusalem. Only incidental references pertain, in the allusion to the tower of David (4.4), the city of Solomon's wedding (3.11) and perhaps in the use of the verb '*lh* in 8.5. No reference is made to the great city of symbolic tradition, the city at the centre of the world (Ezek. 5.5-6), the focus of prophetic hope (Jer. 33; Ezek. 40-48; Isa. 44.26; 52.1; Hag. 2.9; Zech. 2.4, 5) and of eschatological transformation (Isa. 60–61; Rev. 21.1-2). Rather, Jerusalem is eclipsed behind a city without a name, the city of the narratives (3.1-4; 5.7) which is at best indifferent, at worst hostile to the lovers. Jerusalem nevertheless has an important role. Indeed its presence is surprisingly pervasive, thanks to the daughters of Jerusalem to whom are related the events of love. In this way it becomes a kind of redactorial centre, just as the garden is the symbolic centre and the woman herself the focus of the Song.

This final chapter deals largely with the way in which the images of the Song work together, highlighting the fragility of temporal and spatial relationships in what is essentially a emotional drama. We have also noted a paradoxical concern with right timing and a certain urgency on the part of the lovers, in complete contrast with the oneiric atmosphere of much of the Song.

Important too, in spite of the fragility of spatial relationships, is the identification of the lovers with certain milieux, the woman with interior environments and her lover with the spacious outdoors, for it is in terms of thresholds crossed that their longing for unity is realized in such a way as to suspend, for a moment, all boundaries. I refer here in particular to the image of the woman as a garden, for all the beauties of the world in spring are rediscovered in her.

Although the Song depends to a great extent on movement—on the dialogue between the lovers, on his movement to and from her door and on the shifting contours of absence and presence, longing and fulfilment—nevertheless it is powerfully centrifugal, focused upon the woman and the image of the garden which symbolically represents her. In this centring process the daughters of Jerusalem too play their part, for they make Jerusalem the redactorial centre of the Song. It is in this setting that the dialogue comes alive precisely by being related to them.

CONCLUSIONS

What, then, can be said about the different functions of the imagery of the Song at the conclusion of our study? It is time now to review my findings.

First of all, as already suggested, the Song is not a philosophical treatise about love, but rather the experience of love, from the perspective of the woman, which the images first and foremost seek to convey. The images function as metaphors, not primarily for a mystical experience, but for the different emotions aroused by the experience of love. The fragility of spatial and temporal relationships I spoke of in the final chapter is therefore the result of an emotional continuum in which the themes of absence and presence, longing and fulfillment, seeking and finding are explored in the light of the imagination. I noted the important role of fragrance in the blurring of distinctions, for fragrance is precisely capable of making the absent present.

Asserting, therefore, the psychological unity of the Song, we are conscious too of a paradoxical homogeneity and diversity of motifs. A host of images is required for the near impossible task of expressing the incomparable beauty of the loved one, for no single image is adequate to the task. Yet, at the same time, a high degree of homogeneity as regards these images reflects the growing communion of the lovers as repeated motifs and images combine with new elements, drawing them into their sphere of influence. Indeed, in the course of this book it has become apparent that the images belong to three main milieux, the family, nature and the court, and that from these milieux derive a number of imaginative fields. Certain images emerge as key images within this context, gathering round them a cluster of related imagery, images of kingship vis-à-vis courtly imagery, for example. Others reveal the mutual interdependence of these spheres of influence, the imagery of oils and spices, for example, which belongs to the realm of nature, to the luxuriance of the court and simultaneously to both. Others still relate to each other by means of inclusion, the imagery of the garden, for example, which at times is the focus of floral imagery (4.13-14) and at times one element among others in the evocation of a world in spring (6.11).

This brings us to the first important consequence of the coherence of the Song's imagery: the imaginative density or layering which is thereby made possible, for there are among the images of the Song particular motifs which, on account of their context or previous associations, progressively take on an implicit metaphorical meaning; opening up the way to *sous-entendu* and innuendo. In particular, this concerns the flowers and fruit of the Song, especially in association with the language of eating and drinking (2.3; 8.2) which characterizes the lovers' lovemaking. By extension, it also affects the imagery of pasturing, for the image of the flock feeding on lilies (2.16; 6.2-3) is a transposition into the animal world of the image of the man feeding on his loved one, he who himself is so often is referred to as a gazelle (2.9, 17; 8.14).

Certain images, those of vineyard and garden, recur in such a way as to take on symbolic dimensions. Parallel yet divergent images, the vineyard represents the woman in her relations with the external world, while the garden describes her unique relationship with her lover. The vineyard is the image she chooses to speak obliquely about herself in sequences at the beginning (1.6) and towards the end of the Song (8.11-12). The image of the garden, on the other hand, is developed into an extended metaphor at the Song's midpoint (4.12–5.2), in order to describe her lover's longing to lose himself in her plenitude and her invitation to come and eat. The image of the vineyard emerges from the spring scene to speak about her integrity and independence. The image of the garden, on the other hand, becomes the focus of this enthusiastic imagery, suggesting that the woman is, at least for her lover, the focus of the natural world. The powerfully centrifugal influence which the image of the garden exercises at the midpoint of the Song is, moreover, in complete accordance with a general movement towards the centre, for not only does the man move to and from his lover's door, but the perspective of the narration is almost entirely that of the woman. Both images, therefore, do more than simply evoke something of her beauty. In accordance with Wellek and Warren's definition of symbol (1956: 189), they are developed in such a way as to not only describe the woman but also to represent her.

As regards the image of the vineyard, an element of narrativity is important to the constitution of the symbol, for the image draws its symbolic dimensions from a strong contrast between before and after. If the image asserts the woman's integrity and independence in 8.12, it is in direct contrast to the absence of freedom which the same image communicates in 1.6. Moreover, it is in the light of the use of the image in the first instance that we penetrate the enigma of the second. An element of narrativity is present too, though to lesser extent, in the development of the image of the garden, for the extended metaphor of 4.12–5.2, in which its symbolic dimensions come to the fore, tells of the gradual opening of the garden to receive her lover.

Narrativity is most evident in the development of regal imagery throughout the Song, for the movement of this constellation of images tells the 'story' of how the male lover, her 'king', becomes captive to her beauty and how she rises to a position of quasi-queenship by virtue of his love. She, who in the opening verses of the Song is marginalized by the daughters of Jerusalem, is in 6.9 openly acclaimed by the entire female entourage of the king. Indeed, her presence in their midst takes on theophanic dimensions, as is suggested by the imagery of 6.10. This remarkable shift in the use of the regal imagery is swiftly followed, however, by the rejection of the language of kingship; for if throughout the Song regal language is used to evoke the splendour of first one lover and then the other, in the closing verses it is asserted that love is not for sale, even to the most rich and powerful, that is, the king. If the wealth and splendour which accompany kingship are fitting metaphors for the lovers' splendour, they are also the foil against which love reveals its purity.

Images drawn from urban architecture, images of city gates and doors, echo the narrative movement described above. If initially the woman suffers the scorn of the daughters of Jerusalem and the harassment of the watchmen of the city (5.7), in the closing verses it is in terms of urban architecture that she asserts her independence. Indeed the entire constellation of courtly images which gravitate around the key image of kingship throughout the Song participate in this movement, anchoring this rich and diverse imagery in a powerful linear dynamic. The capacity of the shifting images to take on the character of 'story' depends on the resources of the imaginative field described above, for the narrative takes shape in the interaction of images drawn from different aspects of courtly life.

As regards nature imagery, I have noted the interplay of the seasons, the way in which images of spring blend and fuse with those of summer in the fulfilment of natural instincts. Indeed the life cycle of plants becomes a metaphor for the fulfilment of these desires. This movement is more circular than linear, as absence yields to presence in a never-ceasing game of hide and seek. In its own way, however, even this circular movement tells a 'story', for it is by means of this movement that the themes of longing and fulfillment, absence and presence, seeking and finding are explored and the depths of love laid bare. Thus it is that when the woman asserts the power of love over death in 8.7, her words resonate in the reader, thanks to the evocation of love which precedes.

An apparently minor motif, water imagery, is nevertheless characterized by a linear narrative movement comparable to that which we noted as regards the imagery of kingship. The discreet presence of water imagery accompanies and mirrors the growth of love throughout the Song. At the climax of the Song, however, at the point where nature imagery takes on grandiose mythological dimensions (8.7), a surprising reversal takes place and water imagery becomes a foil against which love reveals its power. Like regal imagery, water imagery is exploited to the full only to reveal the inadequacy of all language to speak about love. Images are nevertheless a powerful tool in its evocation, indeed our only means of access to a realm too deep for words.

In addition to and sometimes related to these main functions described above, certain motifs have a particular contribution to make to the Song. We noted an intensification in the use of the imagery of artisanship, for example, accompanying the general swell of courtly imagery. We also noted the role of the motif of the veil in evocation of the woman's hiddenness. The cloak, by contrast, is primarily a dramatic device, peculiar to the narrative of 5.2.

A final remark should be made regarding the feminine bias of the Song. First of all, as suggested above, the entire poem finds its focus in the woman. It is from her perspective that events are narrated, and it is her anxieties and longings, her joys and fears that we are invited to share. It is to the emotional continuum of her psyche that the Song gives access, inviting us to experience her longing in her lover's absence and her joy on his return, for it is her thoughts and feelings which are the primary subject matter of the Song. To her lover's emotions, by contrast, we have no access. It is his words and actions, reported by the woman, which alone speak for him. Moreover, the daughters of Jerusalem have an important role in the evocation of these words and actions, for the experience of the woman is externalized by being reported to them. To them also is issued the warning that love is not to be meddled with, suggesting an educative purpose to the Song. The Song therefore is not simply a meditation on love for its own sake but a kind of *éducation sentimentale* addressed directly to the young women of the community. If the Song evokes the experience of love in order to demonstrate its power, acknowledged openly in 8.7, it is in order to protect these young women lest they open themselves to love too soon. If Proverbs 1–9 warns young men against the advances of the foreign woman, the Song implicitly encourages the young women to be discerning in their response to the advances of young men. Thus it is that integrity and independence are key characteristics of the heroine of the Song.

The sapiential nature of the Song now comes more clearly into focus, but do these remarks indicate anything about the Song's authorship? The feminine bias of the Song is enhanced yet further by the positive role played by the woman's mother, in contrast to the negative portrayal of her brothers and the absence of a paternal figure. These indications together strongly suggest female authorship, a suggestion which however must remain an intuition in the absence, up till now, of confirmatory evidence.

BIBLIOGRAPHY

Albright, W.F.
1963   'Archaic Survivals in the Text of Canticles', in D. Winton Thomas and W.D. McHardy (eds.), *Hebrew and Semitic Studies Presented to G.R. Driver* (Oxford: Clarendon Press): 1-7.
Alonso-Schökel, L.
1963   *Estudios de poética hebrea* (Barcelona: Juan Flors).
1965   'Sapiential and Covenant Themes in Gen. 2–3', in J.L.Crenshaw (ed.), *Studies in Ancient Israelite Wisdom* (New York: Ktav, 1976): 468-80.
Alster, B.
1985   'Sumerian Love Songs', *RA* 79: 127-59.
Alter, R.
1985   *The Art of Biblical Poetry* (New York: Basic Books).
Andreasen, N-E.A.
1983   'The Role of the Queen Mother in Israelite Society', *CBQ* 45: 179-94.
Angénieux, J.
1965   'Structure du Cantique des Cantiques en chants encadrés par des refrains alternants', *ETL* 41: 96-142.
1966   'Note sur les trois portraits du Cantique des Cantiques: Etude de critique littéraire', *ETL* 42: 582-96.
1968   'Le Cantique des Cantiques en huit chants à refrains alternants: Essai de reconstitution du texte primitif avec une introduction et des notes critiques', *ETL* 44: 87-140.
Audet, J.-P.
1955   'Le sens du Cantique des cantiques', *RB* 62: 197-221.
Barthelemy, D.
1985   'Comment le Cantique des cantiques est-il devenu canonique?', in A. Caquot (ed.), *Mélanges Mathias Delcor* (AOAT, 215; Neukirchen–Vluyn: Verlag Butzon & Bercker Kevelaer/Neukirchener Verlag): 21-35.
Bottéro, J., and S.N. Kramer
1989   *Lorsque les dieux faisaient l'homme: Mythologie mésopotamienne* (Paris: Gallimard).
Brenner, A.
1983   'Aromatics and Perfumes in the Song of Songs', *JSOT* 25: 75-81.
1982   *Colour Terms in the Old Testament* (JSOTSup, 21; Sheffield: JSOT Press).
1989   *The Song of Songs* (OTG; Sheffield: JSOT Press).
Brooke-Rose, C.
1958   *A Grammar of Metaphor* (London: Secker & Warburg).

Budde, K.
1898   'Das Hohelied erklärt', in K. Marti *et al.* (eds.), *Die fünf Megillot* (Kurzer Hand-Commentar zum Alten Testament; Tübingen: Mohr).

Burney, C.F.
1908–1909   'Rhyme in the Song of Songs', *JTS* 10: 584-87.

Buzy, D.
1951   'Le Cantique des Cantiques: Exégèse allégorique ou parabolique?', *RSR* 39: 99-114.

Caird, G.B.
1980   *The Language and Imagery of the Bible* (London: Gerald Duckworth).

Camp, C.
1985   *Wisdom and the Feminine in the Book of Proverbs* (Bible and Literature Series, 11; Sheffield: Almond Press).

Caquot, A.
1971   'Anges et démons en Israël', in *Génies, Anges et démons* (Sources Orientales, 8; Paris: Le Seuil).

Carmi, T. (ed.)
1981   *The Penguin Book of Hebrew Verse* (Cambridge, MA: Penguin Books).

Carroll, W.D.
1923–24   'Bittîr and its Archaeological Remains', *AASOR* 5: 77-103.

Chevalier, J., and A. Gheerbrant
1982   *Dictionnaire des Symboles* (Paris: Editions Juppiter).

Childs, B.S.
1979   *Introduction to the Old Testament as Scripture* (Philadelphia: Fortress Press).

Chouraqui, A.
1970   *Le Cantique des Cantiques, suivi des Psaumes* (Paris: Presses Universitaires de France).

Cook, A.
1968   *The Root of the Thing: A Study of Job and the Song of Songs* (Bloomington/London: Indiana University Press).

Cooper, J.S.
1971   'New Cuneiform Parallels to the Song of Songs', *JBL* 90: 157-62.

Davidson, R.
1986   *Ecclesiastes and Song of Solomon* (The Daily Study Bible; Edinburgh: St Andrew's Press).

De Jassy, O.N.
1914   *Le Cantique des Cantiques et le mythe d'Osiris-Hetep* (Paris: C. Reinwald).

De Moor, J.C.
1987   *An Anthology of Religious Texts from Ugarit* (Leiden: Brill).

De Vaux, R.
1935   'Sur le voile des femmes de l'Orient ancien: A propos d'un bas-relief de Palmyre', *RB* 44: 397-412.

Delitzsch, F.
1875   *Commentary on the Song of Songs and Ecclesiastes* (Edinburgh: T. & T. Clark).

Driver, G.R.
1936   'Supposed Aramaisms in the Old Testament', *JBL* 55: 101-120
1974   'Lice in the Old Testament', *PEQ* 106: 159-60.

Edmonds, J.M.
1912   *The Bucolic Poets* (London: Heinemann).

Eliade, M.
1971   *La nostalgie des origines: Méthodologie et histoire des religions* (Paris: Gallimard).

Elliott, M.T.
1989   *The Literary Unity of the Canticle* (Frankfurt: Peter Lang).

Erbt, W.,
1906   *Die Hebräer: Kanaan im Zeitalter der hebräischen Wanderung und Staatgrundungen* (Leipzig: Hinrichs).

Ewald, H.G.A.
1826   *Das Hohe Lied Salomos übersetzt und mit Einleitung, Anmerkungen und einem Abhang* (Göttingen).

Exum, J.C.
1973   'A Literary and Structural Analysis of the Song of Songs', *ZAW* 85: 47-79.

Falk, M.
1982   *Love Lyrics from the Bible: A Translation and Literary Study of the Song of Songs* (Bible and Literature Series, 4; Sheffield: Almond Press).

Fisch, H.A.
1988   *Poetry with a Purpose: Biblical Poetics and Interpretation* (Bloomington/Indianapolis: Indiana University Press).

Fox, M.
1985   *The Song of Songs and Ancient Egyptian Love Songs* (Madison: University of Wisconsin Press).

Freehof, S.B.
1948–49 'The Song of Songs: A General Suggestion', *JQR* NS 39: 397-402.

Fulco, W.J.
1976   *The Canaanite God Rešep* (AOS, 8; New Haven).

Gadamer, H.-G.
1975   *Truth and Method* (ed. and trans. G. Barden and J. Cumming; New York: Seabury).

Gerleman, G.
1962   'Die Bildersprache des Hohenliedes und die altägyptische Kunst', *ASTI* 1: 24-30.
1965   *Ruth, Das Hohelied* (BKAT, 18; Neukirchen–Vluyn: Neukirchener Verlag/Moors).

Gibson, J.C.L.
1977   *Canaanite Myths and Legends* (Edinburgh: T. & T. Clark).
1979   'The Last Enemy', *SJT* 32: 151-69.
1981   *Genesis*, I (Daily Study Bible; Edinburgh: St Andrew's Press).
1984   'The Theology of the Ugaritic Baal Cycle', *Or* 53: 202-19.
1994   *Davidson's Introductory Hebrew Grammar-Syntax* (Edinburgh: T. & T. Clark, 4th edn).

Ginsburg, C.D.
1970   *The Songs and Coheleth* (Library of Biblical Studies; New York: Ktav, 2nd edn).

Goitein, S.D.
1965   'Ayumma Kannidgalot (Song of Songs VI.10): Splendid Like the Brilliant Stars', *JSS* 10: 220-21.
1988   'Women as Creators of Biblical Genres', *Prooftexts* 8: 1-33.

Good, E.M.
1970   'Ezekiel's Ship: Some Extended Metaphors in the Old Testament', *Semitics* 1: 79-103.

Gordis, R.
1969   'The Root *dgl* in the Song of Songs', *JBL* 88: 203-204.
1974   *The Song of Songs and Lamentations* (New York: Ktav, 2nd edn).

Goulder, M.
1986   *The Song of Fourteen Songs* (JSOTSup, 35; Sheffield: JSOT Press).

Graetz, H.H.
1871   *Schir Ha-Schirim oder das Salomonische Hohelied* (Vienna).

Grober, S.F.
1984   'The Hospitable Lotus: A Cluster of Metaphors: An Inquiry into the Problem of Textual Unity in the Song of Songs', *Semitics* 9: 86-112.

Hallo, W.W.
1970   'The Cultic Setting of Sumerian Poetry', in A. Finet (ed.), *Actes de la XVIIe Rencontre Assyriologique Internationale: Bruxelles, 1969* (Gembloux: Duculot).

Haulotte, G.
1966   *Symbolique du vêtement selon la Bible* (Théologie, 65; Paris: Aubier).

Haupt, P.
1902a   'The Book of Canticles', *AJSL* 18: 193-245.
1902b   'The Book of Canticles', *AJSL* 19: 1-21.
1907   *Biblische Liebeslieder: Das sogenannte Hohelied Salomos unter steter Berücksichtigung der Übersetzungen Goethes und Herders* (Leipzig: Hinrichs).

Held, M.
1961   'A Faithful Lover in Old Babylonian Dialogue: Addenda and Corrigenda', *JCS* 15: 1-26.

Hermann, A.
1959   *Altesägyptische Liebeslieder* (Wiesbaden: Harrassowitz).

Honeyman, A.M.
1949   'Two Contributions to Canaanite Toponymy', *JTS* 50: 50-52.

Horst, F.
1935   'Die formen des althebräischen Liebesliedes', in *Orientalistische Studien, Enno Littmann zu seinem 60 Geburtstag überreicht* (Leiden: Brill): 43-54.

Isserlin, B.S.J.
1958   'Song of Songs IV, 4: An Archaeological Note', *PEQ* 909: 59-60.

Jacobsen, T.
1976   *The Treasures of Darkness: A History of Mesopotamian Religion* (New Haven/London: Yale University Press).

1987   *The Harps That Once…; Sumerian Poetry in Translation* (New Haven/ London: Yale University Press).

Jastrow, M.
1921   *The Song of Songs* (Philadelphia: J.B. Lippencott).

Jaussen, A.
1910   'Coutumes des Arabes: Le *gôz musarrib*', *RB* 19: 237-49.

Jobling, D.
1980   'The Myth Semantics of Gen. 2.46–3.24', *Semeia* 18: 41-49.

Joüon, P.
1909   *Le Cantique des Cantiques: Commentaire philologique et exégétique* (Paris: Beauchesne, 2nd edn).

1947   *Grammaire de l'hébreu biblique* (Rome: Institut Biblique Pontifical, 2nd edn).

Jung, C.G.
1971   *Psychological Reflections* (London: Ark Paperbacks).

Keel, O.
1984   *Deine Blicke sind Tauben: Zur Metaphorik des Hohen Liedes* (Stuttgarter Bibelstudien 114-115; Stuttgart: Katholisches Bibelwerk).

1986   *Das Hohelied* (Zürcher Bibelkommentare, AT 18; Zürich: Theologischer Verlag).

Kittay, E.F., and A. Lehrer
1981   'Semantic Fields and the Structure of Metaphor', *Studies in Language* 5.1: 31-63.

Kittay, E.F.
1987   *Metaphor: Its Cognitive Force and Linguistic Structure* (Oxford: Clarendon Press).

Kramer, S.N.
1962   'The Biblical "Song of Songs" and the Sumerian Love Songs', *Expedition* 5: 25-31.

1963   'Cuneiform Studies and the History of Literature: The Sumerian Sacred Marriage Texts', *Proceedings of the American Philosophical Society* 107: 485-516.

1969   *The Sacred Marriage Rite: Aspects of Faith, Myth and Ritual in Ancient Sumer* (Bloomington/London: Indiana University Press).

Krauss, S.
1936   'Der richtige Sinn von "Schrecken in der Nacht", HL 1118', in B. Schindler *Occident and Orient, Moses Gaster Eightieth Anniversary Volume* (London: Taylor's Foreign Press): 323-30.

Krinetzki, L. (=G.)
1964   *Das Hohe Lied: Kommentar zu Gestalt und Kerygma eines alttestamentlichen Liebesliedes* (Düsseldorf: Patmos-Verlag).

1981   *Kommentar zum Hoheslied: Bildsprach und Theologische Botschaft* (Beiträge zur biblischen Exegese und Theologie, 16; Frankfurt: Peter Lang).

Kuntzmann, R.
1983   *Le symbolisme des jumeaux au Proche-Orient ancien* (Paris: Beauchesne).

Lakoff, G., and M. Johnson
1980   *Metaphors We Live By* (Chicago: University of Chicago Press).
Lambert, W.G.
1959   'Divine Lyrics from Babylon', *JSS* 4: 1-15.
Landy, F.
1979   'The Song of Songs and the Garden of Eden', *JBL* 98: 513-28.
1980   'Beauty and the Enigma: An Enquiry into Some Interrelated Episodes of the Song of Songs', *JSOT* 17: 55-106.
1983   *Paradoxes of Paradise* (Bible and Literature Series, 5; Sheffield: Almond Press).
Leech, G.N.
1969   *A Linguistic Guide to English Poetry* (London: Longmans).
Legrand, Ph.-E. (ed.)
1936   Herodote. Histoires Livre II (Paris: Societé d'Edition 'Les Belles Lettres').
Leick, G.
1988   *A Dictionary of Ancient Near Eastern Architecture* (London: Routledge & Kegan Paul).
Lewis, C.S.
1958   *Reflections on the Psalms* (London: G. Bles).
Loretz, O.
1964   'Zum Problem des Eros im Hohenlied', *BZ* NS 8: 191-216.
1971   *Studium zur althebräischer Poesie: Das althebräische Liebeslied. Untersuchen zur Stichometrie und Redaktionsgeschichte des Hohenliedes und des 45 Psalms* (AOAT, 14.1; Neukirchen–Vluyn: Verlag Butzon & Bercker Kevelaer/Neukirchener Verlag).
Lys, D.
1968   *Le plus beau chant de la creation: Commentaire du Cantique des Cantiques* (LD, 51; Paris: Cerf).
Mace, D.R.
1953   *Hebrew Marriage: A Sociological Study* (London: Epworth Press).
Mackey, J.P. (ed.)
1983   *Religious Imagination* (Edinburgh: T. & T. Clark).
May, H.G.
1955   'Some Cosmic Connotations of *mayim rabbim*, "Many Waters"', *JBL* 74: 9-21.
McAlpine, T.H.
1987   *Sleep, Divine and Human, in the Old Testament* (JSOTSup 38; Sheffield: JSOT Press).
McFague, S.
1975   *Speaking in Parables: A Study in Metaphor and Theology* (Philadelphia: Fortress Press).
1982   *Metaphorical Theology: Models of God in Religious Language* (London: SCM Press).
McIntyre, B.
1987   *Faith, Theology and Imagination* (Edinburgh: T. & T. Clark).

Meek, T.
1922   'Canticles and the Tammuz Cult', *AJSL* 39: 1-14.
1924a   'Babylonian Parallels to the Song of Songs', *JBL* 43: 245-52.
1924b   'The Song of Songs and the Fertility Cult', in W.H. Schoff (ed.), *The Song of Songs: A Symposium* (Philadelphia: Commercial Museum): 48-69.
1956   'The Song of Songs: Introduction and Exegesis', *IB* 5: 98-148.
Möldenke, H.
1952   *Plants of the Bible* (Chronica Botanica, New Series of Plant Science Books, 28; New York: Ronald Press).
Morgenstern, J.
1929   'Beena Marriage (Matriarchat) and its Historical Implications (1)', *ZAW* 47: 91-110.
1931   'Additional Notes on Beena Marriage (Matriarchat) and its Historical Implications (2)', *ZAW* 49: 46-58.
Moshe, H.
1961   'A Faithful Lover in an Old Babylonian Dialogue', *JCS* 15: 1-26.
Mounin, G.
1971   *Clefs pour la linguistique* (Paris: Seghers).
Moynihan, E.B.
1980   *Paradise as a Garden* (London: Scholar Press).
Müller, H.-P.
1984   *Vergleich und Metapher im Hohenlied* (OBO, 56; Freiburg: Universitätsverlag; Göttingen: Vandenhoeck & Ruprecht).
Murphy, R.E.
1949   'The Structure of the Canticle of Canticles', *CBQ* 11: 381-91.
1973   'Form-Critical Studies in the Song of Songs', *Int* 27: 413-22.
1977   'Towards a Commentary on the Song of Songs', *CBQ* 39: 482-96.
1979   'The Unity of the Song of Songs', *VT* 29: 436-43.
1981   *Wisdom Literature: Job, Proverbs, Ruth, Canticles, Ecclesiastes and Esther* (FOTL, 13; Grand Rapids: Eerdmans).
1990   *The Song of Songs: A Commentary on the Book of Canticles or the Song of Songs* (Minneapolis: Fortress Press).
Nielsen, K.
1985   *There is Hope for a Tree: The Tree as a Metaphor in Isaiah* (JSOTSup, 65; Sheffield: JSOT Press).
Patai, R.
1959   *Sex and Family in the Bible and the Middle East* (Garden City, NY: Dolphin Books).
Pelletier, A.-M.
1989   *Lectures du Cantique des Cantiques: De l'enigme du sens aux figures du lecteur* (AnBib, 121; Rome: Editrice Pontificio Istituto Biblico).
Pope, M.
1977   *The Song of Songs* (AB, 76; Garden City, NY: Doubleday).
Pouget, G.S., and J. Guitlon
1934   *Le Cantique des Cantiques* (Paris: Gabalda).
Rabin, C.
1973   'The Song of Songs and Tamil Poetry', *SR* 3: 205-19.

Reinhold, H.A. (ed.)
1947   *The Spear of Gold: Revelations of the Mystics* (London: Burns & Oates).

Renan, E.
1860   *Le Cantique des Cantiques, traduit de l'hébreu avec une étude sur le plan, l'âge et le caractère du poème* (Paris: Calman Lévy).

Renger, J.
1972–75   'Heilige Hochzeit', *RA* 2: 251-59.

Richards, I.
1936   *The Philosophy of Rhetoric* (Oxford: Oxford University Press).

Ricoeur, P.
1969   *The Symbolism of Evil* (Boston: Beacon).
1975   *La métaphore vive* (Paris: Seuil).

Robert, A., J.-R. Tournay and A. Feuillet
1963   *Le cantique des cantiques: Traduction et commentaire* (Paris: Gabalda).

Rowley, H.H.
1939   'The Meaning of the Shulamite', *AJSL* 56: 84-91.
1965   'The Interpretation of the Song of Songs', in *The Servant of the Lord* (Oxford: Basil Blackwell, 2nd edn): 195-245.

Rudolph, W.
1962   *Das Buch Ruth. Das Hohe Lied. Die Klagelieder* (KAT; Gütersloh: Gerd Mohn).

Ryken, L.
1974   *The Literature of the Bible* (Grand Rapids: Academie Books).

Sasson, J.M.
1973   'A Further Cuneiform Parallel to the Song of Songs?', *ZAW* 8: 359-60.

Scheinlein, R.P.
1984   'A Miniature Anthology of Mediaeval Hebrew Wine Songs', *Prooftexts* 4: 269-79.

Schmökel, H.
1956   *Heilige Hochzeit und Hoheslied* (Wiesbaden: Franz Steiner).

Segal, M.
1962   'The Song of Songs', *VT* 12: 470-90.

Van Selms, A.
1954   *Marriage and Family Life in Ugaritic Literature* (Pretoria Oriental Series, 1; London: Luzac).

Shea, W.H.
1980   'The Chiastic Structure of the Song of Songs', *ZAW* 9: 378-96.

Simons, J.
1959   *The Geographical and Topographical Texts of the Old Testament* (Leiden: Brill).

Soulen, R.
1967   'The Wasfs of the Song of Songs and Hermeneutic', *JBL* 86: 183-90.

Stienstra, N.
1993   *YHWH is the Husband of his People: Analysis of a Biblical Metaphor with Special Reference to Translation* (Kampen: Pharos).

Stolz, F.
1972   'Die Bäume des Gottesgartens auf dem Lebanon', *ZAW* 8: 141-56.
Tournay, J.-R.
1959   'Les Chariots d'Aminadab', *VT* 9: 288-309.
1988   *Word of God, Song of Love: A Commentary on the Song of Songs* (trans. J.E. Crawley; Mahwah, NJ: Paulist Press).
Trible, P.
1978   *God and the Rhetoric of Sexuality* (Overtures to Biblical Theology, 2; Philadelphia: Fortress Press).
Tromp, N.J.
1969   *Primitive Conceptions of Death and the Nether World in the Old Testament* (BibOr, 21; Rome: Pontifical Biblical Institute).
1979   'Wisdom and the Canticle. Ct 8.6c-7b: Text, Character, Message and Import', in M. Gilbert (ed.), *La Sagesse de l'Ancien Testament* (BETL, 51; Gembloux: Duculot): 88-95.
Ullmann, S.
1962   *Semantics: An Introduction to the Science of Meaning* (Oxford: Basil Blackwell).
1964   *Language and Style* (Oxford: Basil Blackwell).
Vaccari, A.
1947   'Il Cantico dei Cantiei nelle recenti publicazioni', *Bib* 9: 443-57.
Wagner, M.
1966   *Die lexicalischen und grammatikalischen Aramaismen im alttestamentlichen Hebräisch* (BZAW, 96; Berlin: Töpelmann).
Wakeham, M.K.
1973   *God's Battle with the Monster: A Study in Biblical Imagery* (Leiden: Brill).
Watson, W.
1984   *Classical Hebrew Poetry: A Guide to its Techniques* (JSOTSup, 26; Sheffield: JSOT Press).
Wellek, R., and A. Warren
1956   *Theory of Literature* (New York: Harcourt, Brace & World).
Westermann, C.
1974   *Genesis 1–11* (trans. J.J. Scullion; BKAT, 1.1; Neukirchen–Vluyn: Neukirchener Verlag).
Wetzstein, J.G.
1868   'Sprachliches aus den Zeltlagern der syrische Wüste', *ZDMG* 22: 69-194.
1873   'Die syrische Dreschaftel', *Zeitschrift für Ethnologie* 5: 270-302.
Wheelright, P.
1962   *Metaphor and Reality* (Bloomington: Indiana University Press).
White, J.B.
1975   *A Study of the Language of Love in the Song of Songs and Ancient Egyptian Poetry* (Missoula, MT: Scholars Press).
Whybray, R.N.
1974   *The Intellectual Tradition in the Old Testament* (Berlin/New York: de Gruyter).

Widengren, G.
    1951   *The King and the Tree of Life in Ancient Near Eastern Religion: King and Saviour IV* (Uppsala: Universitets Ärskrift).
Wilkinson, A.
    1971   *Ancient Egyptian Jewellery* (London: Methuen).
Winandy, J.
    1960   *Le Cantique des Cantiques, poème d'amour mué en écrit de sagesse* (Paris: Editions de Maredsous).
    1965   'La litière de Salomon (Ct III, 9-10)', *VT* 15: 103-10.
Winling, R.
    1983   *Le Cantique des Cantiques d'origène à St Bernard* (trans. R. Winling; Les Pères dans la Foi; Bordeaux: Desclée de Brouwer).
Wittekindt, W.
    1926   *Das Hohelied und seine Beziehungen zum Ištarkult* (Hanover: Orient Buchhandlung [Heinz Lefaire]).
Wolkstein, D., and S.N. Kramer
    1983   *Inanna, Queen of Heaven and Earth: Her Stories and Hymns from Sumer* (London/Melbourne: Rider).
Wyatt, N.
    1986   'The Hollow Crown: Ambivalent Elements in West Semitic Royal Ideology', *UF* 18: 421-36.

INDEXES

INDEX OF REFERENCES

INDEX OF AUTHORS